VERDICT

The Chronicle
OF THE
O.J. SIMPSON TRIAL

WITHDRAWN

BEATRICE PUBLIC LIBRARY
BEATRICE, NEBR. 68310

VERDICT

THE Chronicle OF THE O.J. SIMPSON TRIAL

An Associated Press Book

By Linda Deutsch
and Michael Fleeman
and the writers and photographers
of The Associated Press

Andrews and McMeel
A Universal Press Syndicate Company
Kansas City

VERDICT: The Chronicle of the O.J. Simpson Trial copyright © 1995 by The Associated Press. All rights reserved. Printed in the United States of America. No part of this book may be used or reproduced in any manner whatsoever without written permission except in the case of reprints in the context of reviews. For information, write Andrews and McMeel, a Universal Press Syndicate Company, 4900 Main Street, Kansas City, Missouri 64112.

ISBN: 0-8362-1446-3
Library of Congress Catalog Card Number: 95-83101

Authors: Linda Deutsch and Michael Fleeman
Editor: Norm Goldstein
Photo Researcher: Maura Lynch
Photo Editor: Chuck Zoeller

All photographs and graphics are the property of The Associated Press and cannot be reproduced in any form without the written consent of The Associated Press.

Attention: Schools and Businesses

Andrews and McMeel books are available at quantity discounts with bulk purchase for educational, business, or sales promotional use. For information, please write to Special Sales Department, Andrews and McMeel, 4900 Main Street, Kansas City, Missouri 64112.

Contents

Foreword

LOS ANGELES (AP) — *The judge in the O.J. Simpson case allowed three reporters to cover part of jury selection after a newspaper complained that one wasn't enough.*

Superior Court Judge Lance Ito had originally allowed only Linda Deutsch of The Associated Press *to act as a pool reporter, providing hundreds of other news organizations with information on the jury selection process.*

"The responsibility this places on the shoulder of even a reporter of Linda Deutsch's high caliber is daunting," the Los Angeles Times *wrote in court papers.*

Ito then agreed to allow Times *reporter Andrea Ford and CNN's Greg LaMotte to join the pool.*

TWENTY YEARS AGO, I arrived at a federal courthouse in San Francisco to cover the Patty Hearst trial, which was being trumpeted as "The Trial of the Century," a bit of hyperbole recently attached to the O.J. Simpson case.

In the pressroom, I encountered a journalism legend, Adela Rogers St. Johns, who had come to give her perspective to the trial of the newspaper heiress turned bank robbery defendant.

"Adela," I said, "What do you think of this? Is it 'The Trial of the Century'?"

St. Johns grimaced and snapped, "Don't be ridiculous. I covered the Trial of the Century. It was the Lindbergh trial!"

Certainly the 1935 trial of the man charged with kidnapping and murdering Charles Lindbergh's baby was a sensation in its time.

At the headline-making trial of Charles Manson and his murderous cult members, I met another journalism icon, Theo Wilson of the New York *Daily News,* who had covered every great American trial since the 1960s Sam Sheppard murder case and ultimately became my mentor and role model. I asked if she thought this was the Trial of the Century, and she offered some advice:

"Professional reporters don't call anything the Trial of the Century any more than great war correspondents call a war the war of the century," she said. "It's just another in a series of great stories. Because it's bigger doesn't make it better.

"And don't forget," she added, "the next trial you cover may be even more exciting than this one."

Theo and I went on to cover many defendants whose prosecutions tempted commentators to extremes. Hearst, Angela Davis, Daniel Ellsberg, John Z. DeLorean were among those who found the moniker "Trial of the Century" attached to their cases.

But never was the term so widely used as in the O.J. Simpson trial.

Perhaps because there were many wide-eyed reporters new to the game or possibly because the TV camera's unblinking eye was trained on it, the case became an incredible sensation.

Now, in the cold light of post-trial examination, the search for significance begins. What did it all mean?

At some point in my long courtroom career I formulated a theory that the courts provided a stage for the greatest morality plays of our time and each high-profile trial mirrored the era in which it occurred.

Manson spoke to the drug-induced horrors of the 1960s, the end of flower power and love-ins, the birth of murderous cults. Angela Davis was a black Communist professor accused of complicity in murder and quickly acquitted in a case with racial overtones.

The Pentagon Papers trial of Daniel Ellsberg and Anthony Russo was the trial of the Vietnam War while the war was still raging. The charge was treason for releasing a classified study of the war, and the trial unlocked secret files revealing a pattern of deception by the military.

The Hearst case focused the world's attention on parents vs. children in an age of generation gaps and showed us post-Vietnam alienation that spawned the Symbionese Liberation Army.

The trial of celebrity automaker DeLorean was symbolic of the 1980s. Rich, handsome and powerful, he had a gorgeous model wife, invented a faster-than-fast car and was charged with trafficking in the drug of choice at the time, cocaine. His defense put government sting operations on trial, and he was acquitted.

The list goes on and on. Now we come to O.J. Simpson. What does his trial mean to society? How will we remember it in years hence?

Perhaps jury reform will be debated in august halls of government, and maybe a few changes will be made.

But beyond the sound and fury generated by battalions of lawyers on both sides who raised issues such as domestic violence and racial equality, the overriding social impact of the Simpson case is likely to be on a public suddenly addicted to daily TV trials as a way of life. Their supply could be abruptly cut off.

A backlash is developing against cameras in the courtroom, and judges are loathe to subject themselves to the kind of scrutiny focused on Judge Lance Ito. Lawyers are reassessing whether they want their own careers battered in public— a process that ended with the defense "Dream Team" caught in an ugly, backbiting dispute.

Life in the courtroom spotlight has become more dangerous than politics.

Reporters who were drawn into the excess of competing with supermarket tabloids may reassess their chosen profession. Oddly enough, my guess is the O.J. Simpson trial will be remem-

bered for the way we covered it and for the way it changed the world of journalism for the people who called it "The Trial of the Century."

Linda Deutsch
The Associated Press
1995

CHRONOLOGY

June 1994 through October 1995

Photo Paul Hurschmann

Chronology

Nicole Brown Simpson

Key dates in the O.J. Simpson case:

1994

June

12: Nicole Brown Simpson and Ronald Goldman stabbed to death outside her condominium.

13: Simpson arrives in Chicago. Detectives go to Simpson's estate and conduct warrantless search. Simpson told of murders and flies back to Los Angeles. Undergoes questioning at police headquarters.

16: Simpson accompanies children Sydney and Justin to ex-wife's funeral; friends and family attend Goldman's funeral.

17: Simpson charged with murder. Failing to surrender as promised, Simpson is declared fugitive. He's later spotted in white Ford Bronco with friend Al Cowlings driving. Police follow for 60 miles across Southern California freeways, ending at Simpson's home, where he is arrested.

Ron Goldman

O.J. Simpson

July

8: After six-day preliminary hearing, Municipal Judge Kathleen Kennedy-Powell finds "ample evidence" for trial.

22: Simpson pleads "absolutely 100 percent not guilty"; case assigned to Superior Court Judge Lance Ito.

27: Goldman's estranged mother files wrongful death lawsuit against Simpson, alleging he "willfully, wantonly and maliciously" killed her son.

30: Grand jury transcripts depict Simpson as jealous man who stalked ex-wife.

Al Cowlings

Christopher Darden

Barry Scheck

Robert Shapiro

F. Lee Bailey

August

18: Defense files motion, later denied, seeking Detective Mark Fuhrman's personnel and military records. Defense sources earlier said they might portray Fuhrman as racist cop who moved bloody glove from murder scene to Simpson's estate.

22: Court papers disclose that some DNA tests show Simpson's blood has same genetic makeup as samples from blood trail leading from murder scene.

September

2: Prosecutors file motion for jury sequestration.

9: Prosecutors announce they will seek sentence of life without parole rather than death penalty.

19: Ito rejects defense claims of sloppy detective work, says police acted properly when they searched Simpson's house without warrant.

26: Jury selection begins.

November

3: Jury of eight women, four men selected. Panel composed of eight blacks, one white, one Hispanic and two people of mixed race.

December

8: Alternate jury selected; nine women and three men; seven blacks, four whites, one Hispanic.

1995

January

4: Defense abandons challenge of DNA evidence.

11: Jurors sequestered; court releases explosive prosecution documents accusing Simpson of beating, degrading and stalking Ms. Simpson throughout their 17-year relationship. Documents are released as hearing begins on defense bid to bar evidence of domestic violence. Defense accuses prosecution of character assassination.

12: Prosecutors withdraw 18 of 62 abuse allegations.

13: At hearing to determine whether defense will be permitted to question Fuhrman about alleged racial slurs, prosecutor Christopher Darden and defense attorney Johnnie Cochran Jr., both black, engage in emotional exchange over role of race in trial.

17: Prosecution documents allege Simpson hit his first wife, Marguerite Simpson Thomas. Officer who responded to domestic call some 20 years earlier says Simpson's then-wife said Simpson hit her and she was taken to hotel for the night. In June police interview, Ms. Thomas denied Simpson ever abused her.

18: Ito rules jurors can hear evidence of domestic violence in Simpson's relationship with Nicole Brown Simpson; dismisses two jurors. After highly publicized bickering between Simpson attorneys Robert Shapiro and F. Lee Bailey, Cochran takes lead on defense team.

20: Ito allows possibility of Fuhrman racism introduced if defense can prove it's relevant.

24: Ito rejects Simpson's request to speak directly to jurors before defense opening statements but allows him to show scars on knees. Darden and prosecutor Marcia Clark begin opening statements.

27: Simpson's book, *I Want to Tell You,* released, responds to more than 300,000 pieces of mail sent to him in jail.

31: First prosecution witness testifies. Sharyn Gilbert, a 911 operator and dispatcher, testifies she answered call from Simpson's home on New Year's Day 1989.

Denise Brown

Patti Goldman

Kim Goldman

Fred Goldman

Marcia Clark

Judge Lance Ito

Johnnie Cochran

February

3: Denise Brown sobs on witness stand as she testifies how Simpson humiliated her sister Nicole in public and once hurled her against a wall.

7: Juror Katherine Murdoch dismissed.

12: Jurors make daytime tour of Simpson's estate and murder scene.

March

1: Juror Michael Knox dismissed.

15: Fuhrman denies under cross-examination he used racial slur in past 10 years.

17: Juror Tracy Kennedy dismissed.

April

5: Juror Jeanette Harris dismissed.

11: Criminalist Dennis Fung testifies and concedes he didn't detect blood on socks at Simpson's home or on back gate of murder scene until weeks later.

21: Jurors wear black to court and refuse to hear testimony, after three deputies who guarded panel are reassigned amid charges of giving preferential treatment to white jurors.

May

1: Juror Tracy Hampton dismissed.

4: Goldman's father and sister file wrongful death lawsuit against Simpson.

10: Testimony about DNA blood analysis begins; scientist Robin Cotton is first witness to link Simpson to murders through genetic tests.

26: Juror Francine Florio-Bunten dismissed.

June

5: Jurors Farron Chavarria and Willie Cravin dismissed. Juror makeup now nine blacks, one Hispanic and two whites; 10 women, two men.

12: Estate of Ms. Simpson files lawsuit claiming that Simpson "brutally and with malice aforethought stalked, attacked and repeatedly stabbed and beat" his ex-wife.

15: Simpson struggles to pull on bloody gloves found at murder scene and his estate. Prosecutors suggest the gloves have shrunk.

Mark Fuhrman

July

6: Prosecution rests.

10: Defense calls its first witness, Simpson's grown daughter, Arnelle.

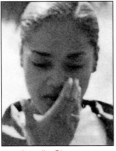

O.J. Simpson

August

15: Clark says she'll ask Ito to remove himself from trial because of appearance of conflict of interest stemming from tapes Fuhrman made with scriptwriter as part of screenwriting project about LAPD. In tapes, Fuhrman makes derogatory comments about Ito's police-captain wife and minorities.

16: Clark backs down from threat. Ito says he'll rule on admissibility of Fuhrman tapes but allows another judge to determine whether his wife is relevant witness.

18: Superior Court Judge John Reid rules Ito's wife has nothing relevant to add to trial.

29: Excerpts of recorded interviews between Fuhrman and screenwriter played with jury absent.

31: Ito rules that jurors will hear only two of 61 excerpts defense wants to present. Cochran calls Ito's ruling cruel and unfair. Lawyer Robert Tourtelot says he will no longer act as Fuhrman's spokesman or represent him in civil matters.

Arnelle Simpson

Tom Lange

Collin Yamauchi

Juror Brenda Moran

Philip Vannatter

September

5: Jurors hear Fuhrman on tape using racial epithet.

6: Fuhrman returns to witness stand, out of jury's presence, and invokes Fifth Amendment protection against self-incrimination. Black witness Roderic Hodge tells jurors that when Fuhrman arrested him in 1987, he used racial slur.

7: Defense ends months of speculation by saying Simpson won't testify. Judge agrees to defense request that jurors be told Fuhrman had become "unavailable" and they could consider that in weighing his credibility. Prosecutors appeal.

8: Appeals court rejects Ito's jury instruction about Fuhrman.

11: Defense refuses to rest case pending appeal of Fuhrman issue; judge orders prosecutors to begin rebuttal.

13: Cochran announces he wants FBI Agent Frederic Whitehurst to testify about problems in FBI crime lab.

14: Appeals court rejects defense request to recall Fuhrman so he can be cross-examined in front of jurors about racist statements in taped interviews.

18: Prosecution conditionally rests.

19: Detective Philip Vannatter is grilled in court about statements he allegedly made to mob informants. Ito blacks out trial for first time in case, so informants can testify. Craig and Larry Fiato and FBI Agent Michael Wacks testify that Vannatter said he suspected "the husband" from the start.

20: Ito bars Whitehurst testimony. LAPD Commander Keith Bushey testifies he gave orders for investigators to go to Simpson's estate and notify him of his ex-wife's slaying.

21: Ito gives jurors option of finding Simpson guilty of second-degree murder.

22: Defense and prosecution rest. Simpson tells judge, "I did not, could not and would not have committed this crime." Ito reads jury instructions.

26: Prosecution begins closing arguments. Ito blacks out trial when court camera inadvertently pans to Simpson's hand as he is writing a note. Judge eventually allows camera back on but fines broadcast group $1,500.

27: Prosecution finishes closing arguments; defense begins.

28: During summation, Cochran upsets Goldman family when he compares Fuhrman to Adolf Hitler. Goldman's father, Fred, tells a live TV audience that Cochran "is the worst kind of human being imaginable." Simpson's family counters with news conference saying, "It's wrong for someone to get up and personally attack our lawyers, and say that they are liars."

29: Prosecution presents rebuttal arguments. Judge gives final jury instructions and the case goes to the jury. A forewoman is selected in about three minutes.

October

2: Jury deliberates less than four hours before reaching verdict.

3: O.J. Simpson is acquitted of all charges.

O.J. Simpson ON TRIAL

June 12, 1994
Nicole Brown Simpson and Ronald Goldman are stabbed to death outside her condominium in Brentwood, Calif.

June 17
O.J. Simpson is charged with murder. Failing to surrender as promised, he flees in his white Ford Bronco, leading police on a 60-mile freeway chase. He returns to his home and is arrested.

July 8
Following a preliminary hearing, a municipal judge rules there is enough evidence to hold Simpson over for trial.

July 22
Simpson pleads "absolutely, 100 percent not guilty."

November 3
The jury is selected.

January 11, 1995
Jurors are sequestered.

January 31
After several weeks of evidence hearings, the first prosecution witness testifies.

July 6
The prosecution rests.

July 10
The defense calls its first witness, O.J. Simpson's adult daughter.

Sept. 22
The defense and the prosecution rest.

Sept. 29
Judge Lance Ito gives final jury instructions and turns the case over to them.

Oct. 2
The jury deliberates less than four hours before reaching a verdict.

Oct. 3
O.J. Simpson found not guilty.

AP

Introduction

Bulletin

LOS ANGELES (AP) OCTOBER 3, 1995, 10:10 A.M. PA-
CIFIC DAYLIGHT TIME—*O.J. Simpson was acquitted
today of murdering his ex-wife and her friend, a suspense-filled climax to the courtroom saga that obsessed
the nation. With two words, "not guilty," the jury freed
the fallen sports legend to try to rebuild a life thrown into
disgrace.*

THE JURY HAD SPOKEN, and the reverbera-
tions would soon explode in a cacophony
that echoed worldwide. It was the end of a
16-month trial that mesmerized the TV viewing
audience and newspaper readers, spawned a raft
of books and created what some called "O.J. Nation," a network of trial addicts connected by
the Internet and by their unique obsession with
one celebrity's fate.

The verdict came so swiftly it left everyone
breathless. Less than four hours to decide a
man's fate and change the course of legal history.
Less than four hours to spin off a national debate
on the meaning of justice, the power of money
and the ability of the public to accept the unac-
ceptable: a murder mystery without an ending.

If the jury was right and O.J. Simpson was not
guilty, then who had committed these grisly
murders and why? If the jury was wrong, what
had deluded them and what did it say about the
justice system?

With one of the most famous men in America on trial, the case had been more carefully
documented and analyzed than any in memory.
Looking backward through the prism of the verdict, the outcome seemed foreordained. Many
lawyers played out their roles in this
national psychodrama. But the man in
control from the beginning was the
defendant, O.J. Simpson.

He was on camera again. All eyes
were focused on the legend who once
mesmerized football fans with his dar-
ing runs. One could almost hear the
roar of the crowd—"O.J., O.J., O.J."

But this time it was no game. His life
was at stake and he knew it. He didn't blink. O.J.
Simpson stood up in the crowded courtroom,
his hulking form dwarfing those around him. As
jurors watched in amazement he quickly pulled
on a pair of latex gloves, then unflinchingly
reached for the two crumpled leather gloves
stained   with   the   blood
of his slain ex-wife.

He walked toward the jury box, tugging
hard at the wrists, holding his arms aloft to show
the gloves not quite covering his large hands.

"They're too small," he said quietly.

Those were the only three words he spoke
to jurors during his entire trial, and they were
enough. There was no need to testify after that.
No need to subject himself to the hostile questions
of prosecutor Marcia Clark. No need to address
the minutiae of where he was on the murder
night. In the eyes of his jurors, O.J. Simpson had

O.J. Simpson as he appeared at the Pediatric AIDS Foundation picnic/carnival,
"A Time for Heroes 1994," on June 5, 1994. Sixteen days later, he pleaded not
guilty to murdering his ex-wife, Nicole Brown Simpson, and Ronald Goldman.

Photo Donna Gilmartin

A family photo of Ronald Goldman.

It was a courtroom moment for the history books and law books. The irony was that Simpson had been asked to try on the murder gloves not by his lawyers but by a prosecutor who gambled that they would fit.

There had been other memorable moments in the long trial and there would be more after this, but the date of June 15, 1995, would stand out as the day the tables turned.

It was just one year since the murders of Nicole Brown Simpson and Ronald Goldman had focused an unwelcome spotlight on the celebrated athlete, toppling him from his pinnacle of wealth and power, transforming him into a murder defendant and thrusting into the hands of the legal system a case of monumental proportions.

In 16 tumultuous months, the saga of O.J. Simpson would focus a searchlight on the soul of American justice and reveal a system stretched to

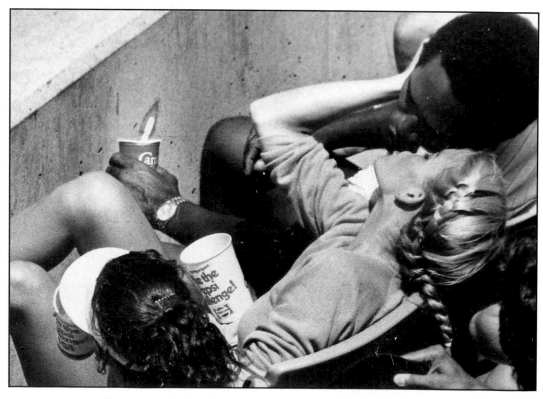

Simpson with his then-fiancée Nicole Brown at a Los Angeles Dodgers baseball game in 1980.

AP Photo

A police investigator walks past blood-stained towels in the entryway to the condominium belonging to Nicole Brown Simpson.

Photo Eric Draper

its limits to cope with the power of celebrity, wealth and an undercurrent of racism so virulent it would be blamed by some for the outcome of Simpson's murder trial. Added to the explosive mix was a seething well of outrage over domestic violence against women and the resentment that

His marriage to Nicole Brown, a blonde all-American beauty, was an interracial union that seemed made in heaven. Nothing bad could ever happen to this golden couple. And then the worst thing possible happened.

In the warm darkness of a June night, on a street in trendy Brentwood, the blood of Nicole Brown Simpson flowed like a river down the pathway of her California condominium. Her beautiful swan-like neck had been slashed open by the knife of a killer—a gash so vicious it nearly decapitated her. Nearby, another body lay oozing blood. Ronald Goldman, a waiter on a mission to deliver a pair of eyeglasses, became the accidental victim in one of the most gruesome murders to grip the public consciousness in decades.

The white Ford Bronco carrying Simpson, driven by Simpson friend and former teammate Al Cowlings, travels the northbound 405 Freeway under the Manchester Boulevard Overpass. Cowlings led police on a two-county chase after Simpson was charged with two counts of murder.

Photo Joseph Villarin

Could O.J. be the killer? No one wanted to believe it.

"I felt sick to my stomach," one juror would recall of hearing he was a suspect. "I couldn't believe it," said others.

And for five days, it seemed that not even the police could believe it. They interviewed Simpson, took a sample of his blood but did not arrest him. The investigation continued. He changed lawyers and consulted with potential witnesses.

And when the time came for him to be arrested on June 17, 1994, O.J. Simpson did what he was famous for—he ran.

With his friend A.C. Cowlings at the wheel of a white Bronco, a distraught Simpson led police—and America—on a bizarre, televised

accompanies the death of a treasured American dream.

O.J. Simpson was the most famous American ever charged with murder: sports legend, movie actor, commercial pitchman, millionaire. With his dazzling smile and startling good looks he was an image of success for black Americans and a symbol of race transcendence for whites. It was safe for everyone to love O.J.

slow-speed chase that wound its way 60 miles across Southern California freeways and set the theme for his trial to come. Justice would be slow, filled with bizarre moments, and all of it would be televised live for a public that could not take their eyes off it.

The man at center stage, who had sent what looked like a suicide note to the world before he fled, came back, surrendered and decided to fight the charges with all the might and money at his disposal.

By so doing he launched not just a legal battle but a national obsession. Never before had a trial of such magnitude been televised live, coast to coast and around the world. And never had the American judicial system been put to such a test. The legal profession, the judiciary and a large cast of individuals sucked into the maelstrom of this all-consuming spectacle were buffeted and left bleeding in the rubble of a publicity barrage unmatched in any courtroom saga past.

The news media itself, messenger of the Simpson case, endured a trial of credibility, seeking to balance ethics with the need to feed an insatiable public appetite for facts—but also for gossip and rumors—about a case that claimed the shorthand nickname "The O.J. Trial."

On July 22, 1994, after a six-day preliminary hearing offered a preview of the prosecution case, O.J. Simpson entered his plea: "Absolutely 100 percent not guilty."

On the way out of court, the defendant, who had appeared dazed and depressed in preceding days, smiled slightly and gave a "thumbs-up"

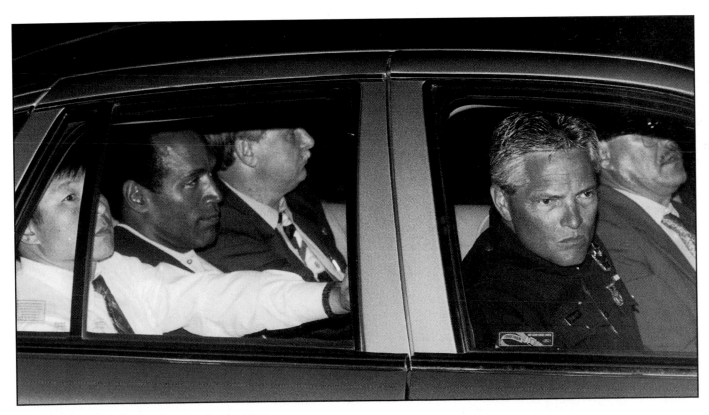

Simpson is driven into Los Angeles police headquarters following his arrest on Friday night, June 17, 1994.

Photo Bob Galbraith

sign to his supporters. The preliminaries were over, and the main event was about to begin.

In the corridors of the Los Angeles County Criminal Courts Building, the buzz had begun immediately about who would handle the case. The wagering was highest on who would represent Simpson, a rich man who could afford the very best. Lawyers across the country burned up telephone lines offering their services. One noted attorney, Howard Weitzman, had bowed out quickly in a dispute with Simpson, and another, Robert Shapiro, seized the case with vigor, recruiting experts and organizing strategy before Simpson was even arrested. But Shapiro, a veteran barrister, was better known for settling cases

Judge Ito in court.

Photo Mark J. Terrill

than for trying them, and he began looking for the courtroom talent to back him up. O.J. Simpson vowed from the outset that he was innocent, and the goal of this defense was acquittal, not settlement.

Broadcasters and legal pundits, spinning off in a whirlwind of hyperbole, were calling this "The Trial of the Century" and predicting that those who stepped in its limelight would have a career-making opportunity. No one could have predicted how badly it would turn out for most of them.

Superior Court Judge Lance Ito, assigned to the case, a cheerful, witty man with a reputation for legal acumen, took on the job with slight reservations but obvious gusto. He seemed the perfect choice. A Japanese-American, he could not be accused of taking sides on the basis of race, and he had already survived one high-profile trial, the financial swindle case of Charles Keating. Ito, one of the brightest judges to emerge from the district attorney's office, seemed an example of moderation on the bench. He also seemed aware of the potential pitfalls ahead.

Just before he was chosen for the case, Ito gave an interview to a legal publication, the *Daily Journal,* and said any judge "would have to be crazy" to accept the Simpson case and subject himself to such intense scrutiny. He also alluded to the media spotlight that could intoxicate anyone, even a judge.

"The sirens of mythology pale in comparison to the allure of seeing yourself on CNN," he said. "The results, however, can be about the same."

It was a prescient comment given what would happen within a few months. Ito, implored by a personal friend in the TV media to grant an interview, sparked a storm of controversy when his talk with the TV journalist was turned into a local six-part series to promote the

Attorney Howard Weitzman bowed out early after a
disagreement with Simpson.

Photo Michael Caulfield

news show during "sweeps week." Ito, stung by
the criticism of those who labeled him "Judge
Ego," declined all further interview requests.

By the time the trial was over, the cheerful
judge had become a grumpy, nearly tyrannical
figure trying to exert an iron hand on a trial spinning out of control. "Sit down! Sit down!" he
would bark at protesting lawyers. Then he
would turn his wrath on the TV cameras,

pulling the plug on more than one occasion
when he felt his rules had been breached. He
grew teary-eyed and said he felt personally
"wounded" when he was forced to defend his
wife, a police captain, and he angrily imposed
heavy fines on lawyers for contemptuous behavior. With his distinctive beard, mustache and
owlish eyeglasses, he was easily parodied in the
media and had to endure the indignity of watching "The Dancing Itos," a group of black-robed
comics depicting him on TV. His face appeared
on T-shirts and other souvenirs of the trial. The
oddest was the "Eat an Ito" Jell-O mold. With

such publicity, his dreams of ascension to higher judicial realms grew more remote by the day.

Prosecutors and defense attorneys fared no better. They were placed under the kind of microscope that has destroyed politicians and altered history. Now, the courtroom was the arena where reputations were skewered, friendships broken, secrets unearthed and lives altered. The career of at least one politician, District Attorney Gil Garcetti, was in cardiac arrest by the end of the case. He had chosen the best and brightest his office had to offer, spent millions of dollars of public funds and failed to win a conviction.

Simpson and his defense team: from left, Barry Scheck, Peter Neufeld, Johnnie Cochran and Robert Shapiro.

Photo Reed Saxon

The human toll was great. The original prosecution team was struck by disaster just after jury selection. Bill Hodgman, a well-liked, amiable stalwart of the district attorney's staff, chosen to counterbalance the more strident personality of Marcia Clark, collapsed from stress and was rushed to a hospital after a particularly bitter courtroom session. He stepped behind the scenes and left the spotlight to the tough, ambitious Clark, a woman whose dogged determination to convict Simpson—even at the cost of questionable legal moves—drew admirers among viewers but placed her in conflict with the judge and defense attorneys. Clark underwent a widely covered fashion "makeover" for TV cameras, but the circles under her eyes deepened, she lost weight, and by trial's end she appeared worn to a frazzle. Her personal life was dragged through

Marcia Clark huddles with co-prosecutor Christopher Darden during the trial.

Photo Eric Draper

tabloid headlines and she became embroiled in a messy custody fight for her two children when her ex-husband claimed the trial was distracting her from motherhood.

Replacing Hodgman in the co-pilot's seat was Christopher Darden, a black prosecutor whose race made him a lightning rod for attacks by Johnnie L. Cochran Jr., the hardball-playing defense attorney who was also black. Cochran, once a mentor and friend to Darden, accused the district attorney of choosing the younger man for the case merely because of his race. Their friendship soured and broke into outright warfare when Darden tried to ban the use of the word "nigger" in the trial, losing out to Cochran's argument that race was an issue that could not be avoided. Darden, an introspective, sometimes

moody man, was so burned out five months into the case that he said he never wanted to practice law again and was ashamed to be part of the trial. When he made the crucial mistake of asking Simpson to try on the murder gloves, he was castigated by legal pundits nationwide. In the final days, he won public acclaim for a heartfelt closing argument but said he probably would never prosecute another case.

The prosecution's vast trial team, which included at least 10 full-time lawyers and assorted technical experts and support staff, saw their future effectiveness damaged by the Simpson case. DNA experts admitted that the validity of their science had been so harshly attacked by a team of defense DNA experts that new cases would be tougher to win. Defense lawyers had been given a priceless course for free, courtesy of TV, on how to undermine DNA evidence.

Attorney Barry Scheck, architect of the defense DNA attack, would say at the end of the case

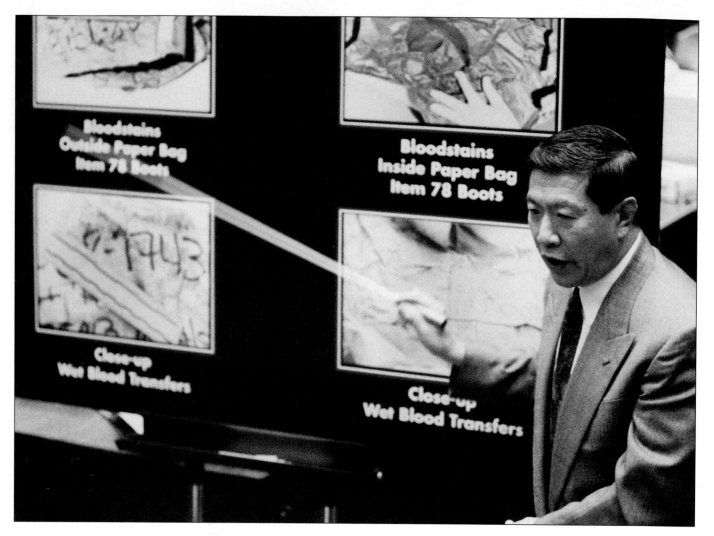

Defense witness forensic scientist Henry Lee uses a pointer as he describes how bloodstains were transferred from evidence items to the paper bags they were carried in.

Photo Reed Saxon

that there were no winners in the long legal battle, an odd statement for one whose client was acquitted. But consider the toll on the defense team:

Johnnie Cochran, who had lived a charmed life as Los Angeles' most revered black attorney, saw his reputation besmirched in grimy headlines emphasizing alleged domestic abuse in his former marriage. His black ex-wife wrote a book castigating him, and his white ex-mistress went public with the story of his double life and illegitimate child. His playing of "the race card" on Simpson's behalf drew widespread criticism, and

some blamed him for widening the racial divide in America. His thundering summation, delivered with the style of a revival preacher, called on the mostly black jury to mete out racial justice. By trial's end, Cochran was receiving death threats and had begun traveling with a retinue of fearsome-looking Nation of Islam bodyguards.

Shapiro, who had organized the defense "Dream Team" and outlined its strategy, was shunted aside as Cochran wrested control of the legal camp. Shapiro's bitter public battle with team member F. Lee Bailey was a personal tragedy, the end of a decades-long friendship. Bailey was the godfather of Shapiro's son, but by the end of the case the two men were not speaking and were attacking each other through the media.

From the day testimony began, it was clear that the O.J. Simpson case would evolve as a tale of two trials: the case in the courtroom before a jury and the contest in the public arena. Outside the courtroom, Simpson's lawyers were playing to a different audience: the public that once embraced the football star and would hold the key to

his future. With talk of a possible hung jury, the defense was keeping one eye on a potential second jury, a group that would likely be chosen from those exposed to the trial on TV. Thus, when particularly sensitive issues came up outside the jury's presence, the arguments were more spirited than ever and often escalated into verbal warfare. The public was watching and the attorneys knew it.

O.J. Simpson, planning on freedom, was looking toward a time when his image would mean everything, and he was counting on his

Los Angeles Police Department Detective Philip Vannatter, foreground, and, from left, Kim, Fred and Patti Goldman, along with Dominique and Juditha Brown, behind the Goldmans, listen to closing arguments.

Photo Reed Saxon

The trail of blood

Genetic fingerprints of O.J. Simpson, Nicole Brown Simpson and Ronald Goldman match bloodstains collected at the scene of the murders and at O.J. Simpson's home. Where matches were found:

At the crime scene

1. **REAR GATE** *Simpson*
2. **SHOEPRINT** *Ms. Simpson*
3. **GOLDMAN'S SHOE** *Ms. Simpson*
4. **MS. SIMPSON'S FINGERNAILS** *Ms. Simpson*
5. **WALK** *Simpson*

At O.J. Simpson's mansion

6. **SIMPSON'S SOCKS** *Simpson, Ms. Simpson*
7. **GLOVE** *Simpson, Ms. Simpson, Goldman*
8. **FOYER** *Simpson*
9. **DRIVEWAY** *Simpson*

BRONCO

10. **Instrument panel** *Simpson*
11. **Inside door** *Simpson*
12. **Steering wheel** *Simpson, Ms. Simpson*
13. **Carpet** *Ms. Simpson*
14. **Console** *Simpson, Ms. Simpson, Goldman (alone or in combination)*

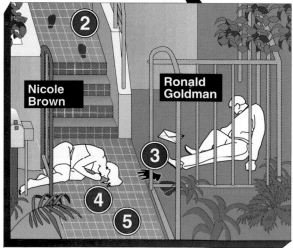

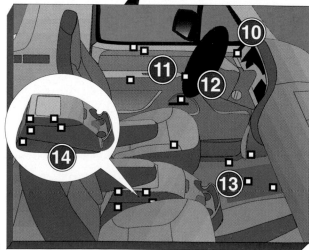

Source: Los Angeles Police Department, courtroom testimony

AP/Karl Gude, Eileen Glanton, Wm. Schroeder

Defense attorney Berry Scheck cross-examines police criminalist Collin Yamauchi.

Photo Kevork Djansezian

lawyers to make that future possible. In the courtroom, they succeeded. Outside the courtroom, the results were dubious.

Many said that the case of *The People* v. *O.J. Simpson* would be won in jury selection, and perhaps it was. The defense had a high-paid jury consultant in court during every day of questioning, reading body language, checking juror questionnaires and advising lawyers. The prosecution's volunteer jury expert appeared only intermittently. With the case tried in the central downtown court district, the pool of potential jurors was racially, ethnically and economically mixed at first. But the bulk of prospects pleaded hardship when they heard

that the trial could last many months and they would be sequestered at a hotel for the duration. This left a panel heavy on civil servants who could afford to serve and retirees who had the time to serve. The pool was predominantly black and so was the final group of 12 jurors and 12 alternates. Shortly after they were sworn in, two were dismissed for failing to reveal pertinent information on their jury questionnaires. And as the trial ground on, jurors began to drop out for assorted reasons. At least two were dismissed for making plans to write books.

The lure of fame and fortune was not far from anyone's mind—least of all the jurors. Eventually, 10 of the original panelists were

Journalists outside the Criminal Courts Building wear Robert Shapiro masks as they await the arrival of Simpson's lawyer on Halloween.

Photo Brennan Linsley

bounced and several rushed to publish their memoirs detailing life inside the world of the sequestered jury. From their accounts, it was evident that the group had broken down along racial lines from the start and for quite a while they were, in the judge's words, "not happy campers." At one point, they wore black and staged a one-day boycott to protest the removal of three deputies guarding them. Toward the conclusion, they sent repeated notes demanding that the trial come to an end. They spent nine months in a hotel that many of them likened to a plush prison.

In court, the jurors were remarkably attentive. And the evidence was perhaps the most elaborate ever heard in a Los Angeles courtroom. Both sides employed high-tech equipment, which the judge nicknamed "the whiz-bang

gizmos," to illustrate their points. There were slides and videotapes projected on a seven-foot courtroom screen and wall-size graphics designed to simplify the confusing crush of scientific evidence. The defense showed pictures of Simpson's unmarked body after the killings; the prosecution showed horrific blow-ups of autopsy photos depicting the slashed necks of Ms. Simpson and Goldman. Some jurors were sickened and had to leave the room. Pictures of the victims' mangled bodies lying in pools of blood became familiar features of the courtroom presentation.

Simpson, who sat at the defense table taking notes most of the time, averted his eyes from the photos. If, on occasion, he caught sight of his ex-wife's butchered body, he would fight back tears.

It was a bloody Grand Guignol sideshow to

a prosecution case reliant on unemotional scientific analysis for its proof. As it turned out, neither the dazzling array of DNA testimony nor the stomach-turning details of the killings, were enough to sway the jurors toward the prosecution's point of view. The panelists were more concerned with alibi evidence, timeline reconstruction and the simple issue of reasonable doubt.

It was, after all, a circumstantial case. No one would come to recount the gruesome killings, for good reason: there were no eyewitnesses save a dog whose plaintive wail in the night was the prosecution's time clock for murder.

There was a large amount of evidence, and for a lesser defendant it might have spelled conviction. But in Simpson's case the burden of proof was elevated, and unanswered questions were magnified by the defense in its bid to persuade jurors that Simpson had been wrongfully accused.

The prosecutors planned their presentation carefully, anticipating the defense points of attack and trying to deflect them before they arose. One thing they did not plan on was the most powerful weapon in the defense arsenal—the defendant's charisma. Without ever testifying, Simpson was his own best witness. Seated at the counsel table in his impeccably tailored suits, he was an imposing, handsome figure radiating an aura of confidence unseen in many who stand accused of such horrible deeds. He was an experienced showman, and his demeanor during the famous glove demonstration showed how quickly he could seize an opportunity and run with it. He did it several times—when he was asked to show jurors the football injuries that scarred his legs and when he displayed his hands up close so they could see his arthritis-swollen knuckles. Jurors were wide-eyed.

If that was not enough to remind them of the old O.J.—the celebrity with the million-dollar smile and the engaging personality—his family filled in the gap. As the defense case opened, the Simpson women came forward to the witness stand. First up was Simpson's grown daughter, Arnelle, a delicate beauty who told jurors proudly that she had been born the day her father won the Heisman Trophy. She was followed by her aunts, Shirley Baker and Carmelita Simpson-Durio, who described their brother's grief after hearing his ex-wife had been slain. Ms. Baker said she applied cold cloths to his brow trying to comfort him.

And, in a scene worthy of a movie, Simpson's frail mother, Eunice, stood up from her wheelchair and hobbled across the courtroom leaning heavily on Cochran's arm to take the witness stand and defend her son. She told jurors of his childhood battle with debilitating rickets and spoke of her own guilt feelings for transmitting the disease when she nursed him. His success as an athlete was all the more miraculous, she suggested.

It was a theatrical but heartfelt display of loyalty from the family which came to court every day to support Simpson's battle for vindication. They believed in his innocence, just as two other families in the courtroom were sure that he was a murderer.

The Browns and the Goldmans, parents and sisters of the two victims, sat before the jury as symbols of grief and loss. As the trial in the media heated up, they became outspoken advocates for his conviction. Fred Goldman, father of Ron, was the most visible, calling press conferences and shedding tears of anger as he railed at the lawyers defending Simpson.

Juditha and Lou Brown, parents of the slain Nicole, had custody of the two younger Simpson children, Sydney and Justin, and their relationship with their former son-in-law and his family was

Simpson declares "I did not, could not and would not" commit murder . The jury wasn't present.

Photo Reed Saxon

ambivalent throughout the trial. Juditha Brown and Eunice Simpson, grandmothers of the same children, often embraced in the courthouse hallway. Once, Mrs. Brown brought a photo album of the youngsters for Mrs. Simpson to see. The Brown sisters, Denise, Tanya and Dominique, often chatted with Arnelle Simpson. Long ago, in another lifetime, they had been loving sisters-in-law. As aunts of the Simpson children, their future lives would be entwined forever.

The trial inside the courtroom sometimes seemed an afterthought to the drama evolving outside. Each morning, participants and members of the media assigned seats in the courtroom would gather in the hallway for a half-hour or so of pre-game chatter. The latest witnesses would be discussed; the previous day's wins and losses evaluated. Then the courtroom doors would open, and a bailiff would announce ceremoniously, "Those with passes for Department 103 may enter now." It was a moment worthy of fanfare music, but there was none, just the hum of anticipation.

Inside court, sides were clearly drawn. The defense sat to the judge's right; the prosecution to his left. Their view of the evidence turned out to be as diametrically opposed as their seating assignments.

Clark and Darden saw the case as a straightforward murder case based on "a mountain" of physical evidence which tied a circumstantial web around Simpson. A bloody crime had occurred, and blood was the key to their presentation. They had the advantage of the space-age science of DNA analysis which, they were confident, would link Simpson's blood type to that of the victims and place him at the crime scene. Clark spoke of a "trail of blood" leading from the scene of the killings to Simpson's estate. Renowned DNA experts gave staggering statistics showing that Simpson was the one person in many billions who could have the same DNA that matched blood found at the scenes.

Darden offered jurors a motive for Simpson to slaughter the woman he once loved—an obsession with possessing her and an unwillingness to let go once they divorced. If he could not have Nicole, Darden suggested, Simpson would make sure no one else did. He used graphic evidence of past domestic abuse to paint a picture of a wife-batterer with an explosive temper. Jurors heard a chilling 911 call made by Ms. Simpson, her voice trembling with fear as Simpson raged in the background. Ms. Simpson's sister Denise wept on the witness stand in recounting incidents which neither she nor her family considered serious until close to the end of Ms. Simpson's life. She said Simpson had humiliated her sister in public and hit her so badly that her face was bruised. Nicole had asked Denise to photograph her as evidence and left the pictures in a safe-deposit box. A Simpson friend, Ron Shipp, said Ms. Simpson told him she was a battered wife, and he electrified the courtroom when he insisted that Simpson had confided to him that he'd had dreams of killing his ex-wife. It was a claim hotly disputed by the Simpson family and by Simpson's lawyers, who attacked Shipp as a liar.

As lawyers intensified their assault on him, Shipp stared across the courtroom at Simpson and sighed, "This is so sad, O.J."

In five months of testimony, the prosecution drew a precise timeline which was designed to ensnare Simpson but may have trapped the prosecutors themselves. It was so precise that a variation of minutes would make it implausible. Could Simpson really have killed two adults, disposed of a murder weapon and bloody clothes, returned to his estate, cleaned up and emerged packed and immaculately dressed for a trip to the airport—all in little more than an hour? Prosecutors said it was possible; the defense poked holes in the timeline from minute one.

The timeline was dependent on two witnesses—both named Kato. Brian "Kato" Kaelin, the nation's most famous houseguest, was the last person to see Simpson before the murders.

Kato the dog, a fluffy brown-and-white Akita, howled a signal of alarm at the killing scene, wandered the streets with bloody paws and led neighbors to the place where his mistress lay lifeless, drenched in blood. Only one Kato could speak on the witness stand. Kaelin, a quirky, would-be actor with a mop of unkempt blond hair, was the prosecution's key witness. And his story was bizarre. He told of accompanying Simpson for a fast-food hamburger that night. He spoke of three mysterious thumps in the night and a small black bag that Simpson personally loaded into a limousine. Kaelin clashed with prosecutor Clark as his halting testimony hinted at a reluctance to implicate his onetime benefactor. At one point, she declared Kaelin a hostile witness.

But phone records and the testimony of a limousine driver, Allan Park, added support for the timeline. Park rang and rang the door buzzer, receiving no answer until he saw a shadowy figure, probably a large black man, enter the house. Only then did the lights go on; only then did Simpson answer the intercom. And within six minutes he was on the doorstep with his bags, appearing every inch the celebrity dressed for the spotlight.

How could he have accomplished this feat in six minutes? It was one of the many points of reasonable doubt that lingered in jurors' minds.

The prosecution was hampered by other deep and abiding problems. Their Achilles' heel was the Los Angeles Police Department, and the defense stuck thorns in it every chance it got. Their laboratory was depicted as "a cesspool of contamination." Their criminalists were shown to be inept if not dishonest. And, in a defense case that cried out for a villain to deflect attention from Simpson, the LAPD provided the perfect foil. His name was Mark Fuhrman and by trial's end he became symbolic of the ingrown attitudes of racism rotting the heart of the LAPD. The veteran police detective was unmasked as a perjurer who lied about using a vile epithet for blacks. The defense discovery of a series of audiotapes in which Fuhrman spouted racist invective was one of the worst blows to Clark. She begged the judge to keep it from the jury's ears.

"This is a murder trial," she argued, "a murder trial where none of this is relevant. This is not the forum . . ." She suggested the case would be derailed by a social issue that would distract jurors from the evidence.

But the defense was adamant; Fuhrman's behavior was central to the case. He was the man who found the bloody glove. He was the man who found blood on the Bronco. He was the man who went over the wall into Simpson's estate when no one answered the buzzer. And now it was clear that he was a racist who had lied under oath about his use of the epithet "nigger."

Judge Ito allowed only fragments of the tapes to be played for jurors, but he permitted incendiary testimony from those who knew Fuhrman as a racist in the past. It was powerful testimony that left jurors biting their lips and the public reeling in outrage.

Those who had dismissed the defense theory of a frameup now thought twice. Maybe it was possible. Maybe Fuhrman did plant the glove. Maybe the blood in the Bronco was his handiwork after all. And what of Detective Philip Van-

natter, who carried Simpson's blood sample in his pocket for three hours, transporting it from the LAPD crime lab to Simpson's estate? A curious state of affairs indeed.

Fuhrman and Vannatter: In his final argument, Cochran denounced them as "the twin devils of deception." They had inadvertently provided the defense with the most important element of its case: reasonable doubt.

For a time it seemed the trial would never end. The defense refused to rest. The prosecution refused to rest until the defense rested. Finally, with the sequestered jury showing fatigue, impatience and intolerance for more testimony, the testimony stopped. The judge asked Simpson to state on the record that he had decided not to invoke his consitutional right to testify in his own defense.

Simpson, seizing another golden opportunity, arose and told the judge, "I did not, could not and would not have committed this crime."

As usual, he was speaking to the world at large. Jurors were absent from the courtroom, but he did not need to address them. They already had gotten the message.

LINDA DEUTSCH
Special Correspondent
The Associated Press
1995

TALE OF THE TRIAL

June 1994 through October 1995

Photo Reed Saxon

June 13, 1994

Los Angeles (AP)

Bloodstained sheets are strewn along the entryway of Nicole Brown Simpson's condominium.

Photo Eric Draper

AN EX-WIFE of Hall of Fame football player O.J. Simpson and a man were found dead early Monday outside her condominium.

Simpson, who lives nearby, was interviewed for several hours by police, but wasn't arrested. His attorney said Simpson was "devastated" and was cooperating with investigators.

The bloodied bodies of Nicole Brown Simpson, 35, and Ronald Lyle Goldman, 25, were found shortly after midnight on a private walkway leading to the woman's West Los Angeles condominium, said Scott Carrier, a spokesman for the county coroner's office.

Authorities have refused to say what time they think the victims were killed.

Simpson spent the day Sunday with his ex-wife and his children, then caught a flight for Chicago at about 11 P.M., his attorney, Howard Weitzman, said. Shortly after he arrived in Chicago, police called him at his hotel to tell him his ex-wife was dead and ask him to return to Los Angeles.

Simpson was briefly handcuffed at his home before being taken away by police.

"I know nothing," he said, looking grim as he got into a car that left for police headquarters about noon.

Asked if Simpson was a suspect, Police

The fatal wounds

Before O.J. Simpson was ordered to stand trial for the murders of his ex-wife and her friend, a medical examiner detailed their wounds.

Schematic drawings

Nicole Simpson's wounds

▶ Simpson died of a knife wound to the neck.

▶ The wound severed both carotid arteries, which supply blood to the head, and one jugular vein, which returns blood to the heart from the head.

▶ The wound went a quarter-inch into one of her vertebrae.

▶ Simpson had four smaller wounds on her neck, three cuts on the back of her head and a bruise on the right side of her scalp.

Ronald Goldman's wounds

▶ Goldman had several wounds that were deemed fatal, either individually or in combination.

▶ A 4-inch-long wound on his right side pierced his lung and nicked the back of his rib cage. A separate 1 1/2-inch-long wound also cut the rib cage and right lung.

▶ A wound to the left flank penetrated 5 1/2 inches and cut the abdominal aorta, the lower section of the body's largest artery.

Both Simpson and Goldman had "defense wounds," sustained in an effort to fight an attacker or seize a weapon.

AP/E. Glanton, R. Toro

markers in Simpson's driveway, marking small reddish-brown stains leading up the driveway to a point about 50 feet from the garage. Simpson's black Rolls-Royce was parked in the driveway.

Police did not say what they thought the stains were.

Simpson spoke with authorities for about 3½ hours before leaving police headquarters with Weitzman.

"We are done for the day," Weitzman said. "We came here to cooperate. We did that. There is a continuing investigation. If we are asked to come back, we intend to cooperate."

Simpson, 46, didn't speak with reporters as he left.

"He is in shock, he is devastated. He had a tremendous amount of feeling for Nicole. . . . It's a tremendous loss," Weitzman said.

In 1989, Simpson pleaded no contest to wife-beating and was fined $700 and ordered to perform community service.

Cmdr. David Gascon said: "We are not going to rule anyone out.

"Obviously we will be interviewing everyone that we think is remotely involved in this case," Gascon said at a news conference. "Everyone is a witness at this point."

At the condo, authorities used towels to soak up blood along the secluded walkway where the bodies were found.

"We feel as though sharp-force injuries played a part" in the deaths, Carrier said. He said that description could include stabbing.

At Simpson's estate about two miles away, police placed cardboard

Simpson after being questioned by police.

Photo Nick Ut

He allegedly screamed, "I'll kill you" as he slapped and kicked Nicole Simpson, his second wife.

Simpson and his ex-wife filed for divorce in 1992 but friends said they recently discussed getting back together. They have two children.

"They were going to get back together. At least that's what I thought," said Carrie McNitt, a former teacher of the couple's 6-year-old son, Justin.

Police said they found two young children asleep inside the condominium but declined to identify them. The Simpson children were staying with relatives, police said at Monday's news conference.

Also Monday, a woman who identified herself as a friend of Mrs. Simpson ran down the street outside the condo, chased by reporters. "Leave me alone. I don't know who did it. Leave me alone," she said tearfully.

Simpson (#32) as a Buffalo Bill.

AP Photo

In recent years Simpson has worked as a network TV sports commentator and has appeared in commercials and several motion pictures including the three "Naked Gun" movies.

He became nationally known as a junior at the University of Southern California in 1967. The following year he won the Heisman Trophy, given to college football's outstanding player.

The Buffalo Bills made him their first-round draft choice the following year, and he quickly became a National Football League star.

After leading the Bills in rushing for nine straight seasons, he played two years for the San Francisco 49ers. He retired in 1979.

Simpson retired from football in 1979. At the time, he played for the San Francisco 49ers.

AP Photo

Nicole Brown Simpson—Profile

Nicole Brown Simpson's Advice:
"Be Yourself"

That simple philosophy appears next to a yearbook picture of a fun-loving senior with blonde hair feathered and parted in the middle, very much the "in" style in 1976.

Her friends called her Nick. The world would later know her as Nicole Brown Simpson.

Within a year of graduating from high school, Nicole's independent spirit was tamed by O.J. Simpson—the dashing football star who swept her out of suburbia and into a jet-set existence that focused on *his* life, *his* friends and *his* career.

It would take years of a physically abusive relationship for Nicole to finally break away from her domineering ex-husband and regain a life to call her own. The decision came just weeks before she and a friend were murdered outside her Brentwood condo.

Nicole's life began almost a half-world away in Frankfurt, Germany, where she was born to an American military man and German mother. The family moved to Southern California after the father's service ended, finally settling in the seaside community of Dana Point.

Nicole's outgoing personality got her voted homecoming princess at Dana Point High School. Her yearbook adage to "be yourself" was followed by a comment that she was interested in photography.

But any hope of pursuing such a career was short-lived. After graduating and becoming a waitress at a Beverly Hills nightclub called the Daisy, she met Simpson and the couple quickly became inseparable.

"She met up with O.J. when she was really young," classmate Mike Cruickshank said. "And that's the last we ever heard of her."

Nicole failed to gain a college education, she said in divorce papers, because of the demands of Simpson's career.

"I only attended junior college for a very short time because (O.J.) wanted me to be available to travel with him whenever his career required him to go to a new location, even if it was for a short period of time," she said.

In 1985, the two were married and the next year Nicole gave birth to daughter Sydney. Son Justin was born in 1988.

Their abusive relationship went public when, on New Year's Day 1989, the now-infamous beating occurred, ending with Simpson's plea of no contest to spousal battery.

It would take three more years before Nicole filed for divorce, after which, her friends say, her life revolved around shuttling her kids to school, taking daily runs along the tree-lined streets of Brentwood and dressing up for nights on the town with her girlfriends. Thursday nights were set aside for Renaissance, a trendy Santa Monica club where she often would run into Ronald Goldman, the friend slain with her.

"Nicole danced up a storm," club co-owner Philip Cummins said. "She was really good about dancing with any guy who would ask. Someone of her beauty, that's unusual."

Underneath her party veneer, Nicole, at 35, was thinking seriously about her future and struggling to regain her independence. Since her divorce, there were attempts at reconciling, but she decided to put an end to that hope.

During the last dinner with her family, the night of her death, she spoke about resurrecting her childhood dream of becoming a photographer, said her sister, Denise Brown.

According to sister Dominique Brown, "That night, (Nicole said), 'Everything is going to change and we're going to be happy,' and we had all decided to spend a lot more time together."

Nicole also indicated that she was ready to move on with her life in a literal sense. Three days before her death, she listed her condo for lease for $4,800 a month.

Nicole's state of mind near the time of her death was perhaps summed up best by her mother:

"She was 18 when she met him, and he was her daddy all along telling her what to do," Juditha Brown said of Simpson in an interview with ABC. "I think what really happened was she grew up."

Nicole Brown Simpson.

AP Photo

Ronald Goldman—Profile

**Had Dreams of
Opening a Restaurant**

Living Day-to-Day

Outgoing and cocky. Adventurous, yet relaxed. This, in his own words, was Ronald Goldman.

He was more than just a waiter. More than just Nicole Brown Simpson's friend. More than just a name in a headline.

After moving from suburban Chicago at age 18, Goldman basked in the Southern California lifestyle, learning to surf, becoming a health club regular, playing softball on Sundays, hanging out at coffee shops by day and hitting trendy spots by night.

"He was always having fun," says longtime friend Mike Pincus. "He lived day-to-day."

On the July weekend that would have marked his 26th birthday, his friends gathered at a Santa Monica nightclub and held a party for him.

"They actually brought out a cake," said Philip Cummins, co-owner of Renaissance. There were "50 guys crying their eyes out."

The tearful gathering is testimony to the affable nature that was indicative of Goldman— a smooth-talking, golden-skinned waiter who boosted his income as a club promoter and occasionally as a model.

A picture of a handsome, bespectacled Goldman is still featured in a fashion ad in a local Cheesecake Factory menu.

Symbolic of his attitude was an appearance on the risqué TV dating show "Studs," for which Goldman wrote the description of his personality in 1991: "Outgoing, cocky, adventurous, relaxed and athletic."

After dropping out of college, Goldman lived with his family in suburban Agoura Hills and held a string of jobs waiting tables, hoping to gain enough experience so he could open his own restaurant, said his father, Fred Goldman.

"That's why he had jobs at restaurants. He was getting a handle on what it took," his father said. "He was putting his life together."

Goldman's drawback, if any, was a penchant for the nicer things in life—a desire that led him to overuse his credit cards so much that he filed

Kim Goldman at the unveiling ceremony for her brother Ronald's gravestone.

Photo Kevork Djansezian

The Goldman family several days after Ronald Goldman was murdered.

Photo Tara Farrell

for bankruptcy in 1992, claiming $12,216.97 in liabilities.

The suburban life soon proved too inhibiting, and Goldman set his sights on Brentwood, a fashionable Westside area where he could hobnob with the rich and famous.

Goldman, however, had little money and no car. He moved to one of the few streets lined with modest apartment buildings, many inhabited by students attending the nearby University of California, Los Angeles. His good looks and his connections in the community often got him into the hottest clubs for free.

At times, he shared his one-bedroom apartment with Jacqui Bell, a clothing boutique worker who ended their on-again, off-again relationship but still held out the hope that someday they might marry.

In Brentwood, Goldman found himself surrounded by a clique of well-toned, youthful bodies who hung out at a Starbucks coffee shop that sits on a bustling boulevard, across from the Mezzaluna restaurant where Goldman worked and Nicole Brown Simpson often dined.

It was at Starbucks, friends say, where Goldman and Ms. Simpson first met, several months before their lives came to a savage end on the pathway of her condo. She often stopped at the coffee shop after a run around town, sometimes with her Akita dog in tow.

Goldman and Ms. Simpson became friends, working out at a pricey gym, driving around in her white Ferrari and hanging out on Thursday nights at Renaissance, where Ms. Simpson usually went with her girlfriends.

The friendship ultimately cost Goldman his life when he offered to return a pair of glasses Ms. Simpson's mother had left at Mezzaluna, where her family had dined that night. It was an errand his friends say was entirely in character.

"He would open his heart to anyone," Pincus says. "You'd ask him for a favor and he would do it."

I KNOW HOW MUCH IT HURTS NICOLE AND I HAD A GOOD LIFE TOGETHER, ALL THIS PRESS TALK ABOUT A ROCKY RELATIONSHIP WAS NO MORE THAN WHAT EVER LONG TERM RELATIONSHIP EXPRIENCES, ALL HER FRIENDS WILL CONFIRM THAT IV BEEN TOTALLY LOVING AND UNDERSTANDING OF WHAT SHE'S BEEN GOING THROUGH. AT TIMES I'V FELT LIKE A BATTERED HUSBAND OR BOYFRIEND BUT I LOVED HER, MADE THAT CLEAR TO EVERYONE AND WOULD TAKE WHATEVER TO MAKE UJ WORK.

DON'T FEEL SORRY FOR ME. I'V HAD A GREAT LIFE MADE GREAT FRIENDS. PLEASE THINK OF THE REAL O.J. AND NOT THIS LOST PERSON.

THANK FOR MAKING MY LIFE SPECIAL I HOPE I HELP YOURS.

PEACE + Love

O.J. ☺

June 17, 1994

Los Angeles (AP)

O.J. SIMPSON WAS HUNTED DOWN and captured in his driveway Friday night after running from charges of murdering his ex-wife and her male friend and leading police along 60 miles of freeways and city streets.

"I can't express the fear I had that this matter would not end the way it did," said Simpson's attorney, Robert Shapiro, who had worried earlier that the former football great would kill himself.

Outside the walls of Simpson's estate, members of Simpson's family hugged each other and cried after word of the arrest came out.

A cheer came up from the crowd of 300 spectators.

The arrest shortly before 9 P.M. culminated an incredible drama that unfolded on live national TV in which police first announced charges against the ex-NFL star, then said he had disappeared and finally followed him along the highways for more than an hour.

After the white Ford Bronco came to a halt at Simpson's estate, a man believed to be his lifelong friend and teammate, Al Cowlings, got out.

The last page of one of three letters written by Simpson and read by Robert Kardashian during a news conference at Shapiro's office.

Photo Mark J. Terrill

Simpson's lawyer arrived at the mansion nearly an hour later and the arrest came minutes later.

Before fleeing as he was about to be arrested, the former football great left a handwritten letter proclaiming his innocence, saying good-bye to friends and making "a last wish" to "leave my children in peace."

Shapiro earlier said he feared Simpson was suicidal and pleaded with him to give up. At the

Even reporters covering the NBA Finals at New York's Madison Square Garden were glued to the television to watch live coverage of Simpson being driven around the Los Angeles area in his white Ford Bronco.

Photo Ron Frehm

same news conference, a friend read Simpson's letter.

"I've had a great life, great friends," the football Hall of Famer's letter said. "Please think of the real O.J. and not this lost person."

The district attorney called it "the fall of an American hero," and Los Angeles police, angered that he reneged on a promise to surrender earlier in the day, mounted a manhunt for him and a former teammate.

In the letter, Simpson wrote that he tried to do "most of the right things" in life and asked: "Why do I end up like this?"

"First, everyone understand, I had nothing to do with Nicole's murder," Simpson's letter begins. "If we had a problem, it's because I loved her so much.

"I don't want to belabor knocking the press, but I can't believe what is being said. Most of it is totally made up. I know you have a job to do, but as a last wish, please, please, please, leave my children in peace," he wrote.

Shapiro said Simpson has been "exceedingly

Simpson and Al Cowlings in 1970.

AP Photo

A dramatic chase

O.J. Simpson disappeared Friday after being charged with two counts of murder. Later in the day, Simpson led police on a 60-mile chase through freeways and city streets. Police believe he had a gun to his head during the chase. The ordeal ended with his arrest at his Brentwood home.

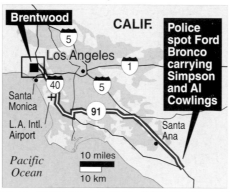

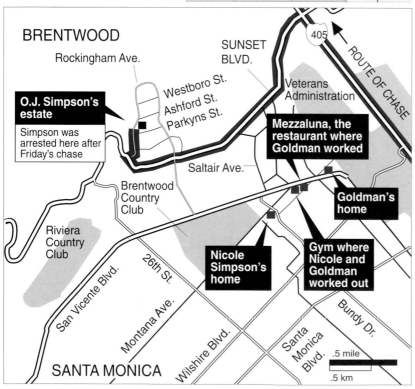

AP

depressed," but he didn't know if Simpson had committed suicide.

"I'm keeping my fingers crossed and praying that we will be able to bring him into a court," Shapiro said.

"Wherever you are, for the sake of your family, for the sake of your children, please surrender immediately."

Police immediately mounted a manhunt when Simpson fled, and said he might be armed.

"Mr. Simpson is out there somewhere and we will find him," Police Cmdr. David Gascon told reporters.

If convicted of killing Nicole Simpson and Ronald Goldman, Simpson—among the most prominent celebrities ever charged with murder—could face the death penalty.

"We saw, perhaps, the fall of an American hero," District Attorney Gil Garcetti said.

Simpson, 46, was scheduled to surrender at 11 A.M. but failed to honor the agreement made with Shapiro, Gascon said.

Shapiro said he was with Simpson, Cowlings and two doctors in a house in

Simpson arrives with daughter Sydney and son Justin at the funeral for Nicole Brown Simpson in Brentwood.

Photo Eric Draper

the San Fernando Valley on Friday morning when police called to say they were coming to arrest him. He said Simpson and Cowlings, who grew up with Simpson in a San Francisco housing project and was his teammate in high school, at the University of Southern California and with the Buffalo Bills, vanished before police arrived.

"The Los Angeles Police Department is actively searching for Mr. Simpson," Gascon said. "The Los Angeles Police Department is also very unhappy with the activities surrounding his failure to surrender."

Authorities also were looking for Cowlings, Garcetti said, warning, "If you assist him in any way you are committing a felony."

The investigation was anchored by a grisly array of evidence, from media reports of a blood-stained ski mask to a bloody glove.

Gascon declined to say how the police lost Simpson, who was handcuffed and questioned by police Monday but let go. He had been seen at his house earlier in the week and attended his ex-wife's funeral Thursday. Someone resembling Simpson was seen driving away from his house an hour before his expected surrender.

Mike Botula, a spokesman for Garcetti, said the charges included the special capital punishment circumstance of multiple killings. There is no bail in such cases, Botula added.

"A final decision on whether we would seek

Thomas Johnson of San Diego autographs one of the many signs in support of Simpson at the front gate of Simpson's house.

Photo Kevork Djansezian

the death penalty will be made at a later time," Botula said.

Fans and colleagues of the sports legend who had insisted on his innocence were forced by Friday's arrest warrant to confront an ominous possibility—that Simpson could have killed the mother of their two children, daughter Sydney, 9, and son Justin, 6.

"There's nothing to say except that the law must take its course," said Howard Cosell, who worked with Simpson on ABC's "Monday Night Football."

The bodies of Mrs. Simpson, the football star's strikingly beautiful ex-wife, and Goldman, a 25-year-old aspiring model and waiter at a trendy restaurant, were found outside Mrs. Simpson's posh condominium.

Mortally wounded by multiple stab wounds, the bodies were discovered in a pool of blood by a passerby.

The couple divorced in 1992 following a seven-year marriage. While still married, Mrs. Simpson called police in 1989 saying she feared he was going to kill her. She had been punched, slapped and kicked by Simpson, who pleaded no contest in the case, authorities said.

Some reports suggested the two were attempting to reconcile at the time of the slayings. They had recently been seen together, but a family friend said those attempts failed and Simpson had turned vengeful.

"He was telling her girlfriends and her that if he ever caught her with anyone he would kill her," the friend told *The Associated Press*, speaking on condition of anonymity. "She totally broke it off with him three weeks ago."

Through his attorneys, Simpson maintained his innocence, claiming he was at home at the

The booking mug for Simpson. It was taken Friday, June 17, 1994.

AP Photo/Los Angeles Police Department

time of the slayings, waiting for a limousine to take him to the airport for a flight to Chicago. He attended his wife's funeral Thursday and hired forensic experts to assist in his defense.

Simpson flew to Chicago the night of the killings and was summoned home by police the next morning.

July 22, 1994

Los Angeles (AP)

Ito's rulings

Superior Court Judge Lance Ito's first few pre-trial rulings in the O.J. Simpson case hit on several highly charged issues. Some key points:

A plus for the prosecution

Ito ruled that the prosecution does not have to share its samples of Simpson's blood. Any leftover samples, however, will go to the defense.

A minus for the media

Ito barred reporters from a hearing on whether an ongoing grand jury investigation of Simpson's friend A.C. Cowlings is acceptable.

A plea for a fair trial

On August 12, 1995 Ito prevented reporters from viewing an especially gruesome photo of the murder victims, saying exposure would jeopardize Simpson's right to a fair trial.

AP/Bob Bianchini

OJ. SIMPSON TOLD HIS STORY in body language as he strode into court, signaled thumbs-up to his supporters and exuded a confidence unseen since his arrest on murder charges.

It was a reborn Simpson at Friday's arraignment, no longer the dazed defendant who could barely utter his name at his first court appearance a month ago. Here was the O.J. his fans had known and loved for decades—a man who looked like a winner.

When the door from his holding cell opened,

The Simpson trial was news—and good copy—for more than a year.

Photo Nick Ut

A sign posted one block south of the murder scene.

Photo Michael Caulfield

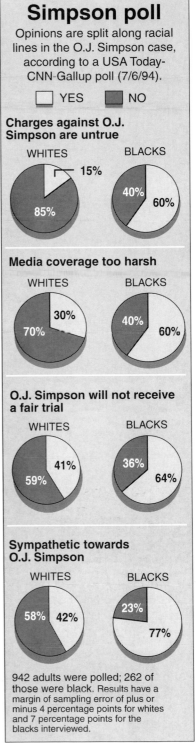

Simpson poll

Opinions are split along racial lines in the O.J. Simpson case, according to a USA Today-CNN-Gallup poll (7/6/94).

☐ YES   ■ NO

Charges against O.J. Simpson are untrue

WHITES   BLACKS

15%

85%   40%   60%

Media coverage too harsh

WHITES   BLACKS

30%   40%

70%   60%

O.J. Simpson will not receive a fair trial

WHITES   BLACKS

41%   36%

59%   64%

Sympathetic towards O.J. Simpson

WHITES   BLACKS

58% 42%   23%

77%

942 adults were polled; 262 of those were black. Results have a margin of sampling error of plus or minus 4 percentage points for whites and 7 percentage points for the blacks interviewed.

AP

and the TV camera rolled, it was clear that Simpson knew he was on. Asked for his plea in the June 12 slashing deaths of ex-wife Nicole Brown Simpson, 35, and her friend Ron Goldman, 25, the former sports star and actor delivered his one line with feeling: "Absolutely, 100 percent not guilty."

His plea followed a week of legal and public relations maneuvers designed to show he has been falsely accused of the two murders. Prosecutors have not decided whether to seek the death penalty.

The nationally televised hearing brought Simpson a step closer to what promises to be one of the most closely watched trials in history. The next step is a hearing Monday before Superior Court Judge Lance Ito, who was selected Friday to preside over the trial.

Ito will hear the defense's request to conduct its own tests on blood samples before the prosecution performs genetic fingerprinting tests, which could use up the samples. Those tests are scheduled to begin Tuesday.

Ito also will hear a defense motion demanding that authorities turn

Curious onlookers and tourists began flocking to Simpson's house shortly after Simpson was arrested.

Photo Chris Pizzello

The Simpson case
The accused

Orenthal James Simpson

Arrested on two counts of murder, with a provision that allows for the death penalty. A Hall of Fame football player, "O.J.," 46, rose to National Football League fame and launched a successful second career as an actor and sports broadcaster.

The victims

Nicole Brown Simpson

Married O.J. in 1985. Together, they had a daughter, 9, and a son, 6. She complained several times of spousal abuse, and in 1992, divorced Simpson. Nicole, 35, continued to see her ex-husband, but was often spotted out in Los Angeles.

Ronald Goldman

The 25-year-old waiter at Mezzaluna, where Nicole Simpson dined the night of the murders, also modeled occasionally. He knew Nicole from the restaurant, and they worked out at the same gym, but the depth of their relationship is unclear.

AP/Tracie Tso, R. Kowlessar

over virtually all reports and leads linked to the case. Simpson's lawyers argued that prosecutors were so eager to bag a celebrity that they ignored evidence that could exonerate him.

Simpson appeared more confident and stronger Friday than at previous court appearances. He strode into the courtroom, shook hands with his two lawyers and shared comments with them before the hearing began.

He even gave a thumbs-up sign to friends in the spectator section as he was hauled back to his holding cell.

It was a far cry from the bedraggled Simpson who was barely able to mutter his own name at a Municipal Court arraignment June 20, and who wasn't allowed to wear a tie, shoelaces or belt because authorities feared he might kill himself.

Also Friday, Simpson's defense team took on Johnnie Cochran Jr., a well-respected trial attorney whose clients have included Michael Jackson.

"He is one of the finest trial lawyers in Los Angeles, and he has a remarkable legal mind. His temperament is just perfect for this case," said attorney Edi Faal, who represented one of the men accused of beating trucker Reginald Denny.

Cochran's addition also gives the Simpson team its first black lawyer and someone with close ties to local black leaders.

That's important because race could become an issue in the case. Members of the defense team have said they may try to show that a white police detective framed Simpson by planting a bloody glove at his estate.

"In a multiethnic city, with a multiethnic jury, race is another factor you have to take into consideration," said civil rights attorney Leo J. Terrell. "Being an African-American, it will have a favorable impression on African-American jurors."

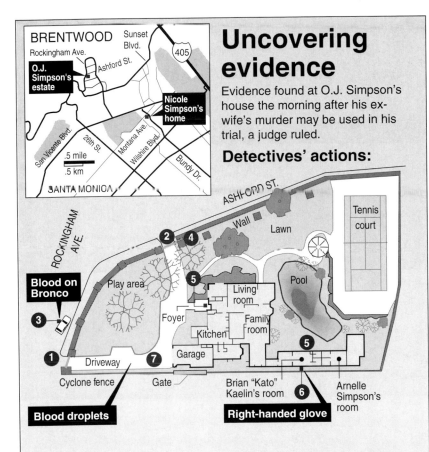

Uncovering evidence

Evidence found at O.J. Simpson's house the morning after his ex-wife's murder may be used in his trial, a judge ruled.

Detectives' actions:

BRENTWOOD — Sunset Blvd. — Rockingham Ave. — 405 — Ashford St. — O.J. Simpson's estate — Nicole Simpson's home — San Vicente Blvd. — 26th St. — Montana Ave. — Wilshire Blvd. — Bundy Dr. — .5 mile — .5 km — SANTA MONICA

ASHFORD ST. — Wall — Lawn — Tennis court — ROCKINGHAM AVE. — Play area — Living room — Pool — Blood on Bronco — ③ — Foyer — Family room — Kitchen — Garage — Driveway — ① — ⑦ — Cyclone fence — Gate — Brian "Kato" Kaelin's room — ⑥ — Arnelle Simpson's room — ② ④ ⑤ ⑤

Blood droplets   **Right-handed glove**

❶ Detectives Mark Fuhrman, Philip Vannatter, Tom Lange and Mark Phillips arrive at O.J. Simpson's mansion at 360 Rockingham Ave. shortly after 5 a.m. June 13.

❷ A ring of the intercom buzzer goes unanswered. Lights are on in the house.

❸ Fuhrman says a white Ford Bronco, parked haphazardly outside the estate, has a speck of blood on the driver's side door handle. He asks Vannatter to inspect the Bronco.

❹ Vannatter calls for a criminalist and decides to go over the wall. Fuhrman scales the 5-foot wall and unlocks the gate for the others.

❺ Detectives ring the bell at the front door; there is no answer. At about 5:30 a.m., they knock at the doors of houseguest Brian Kaelin and Simpson's daughter Arnelle, 25. Arnelle admits the detectives and tries to locate her father by telephone.

❻ Kaelin tells detectives he heard a thumping noise the previous night. Between 6 and 6:15 a.m., Fuhrman goes to a backyard path to investigate and discovers a bloody right-handed brown leather glove, which matches a left-handed glove found at the murder scene. Over the next 40 minutes, he calls the other detectives back one by one to examine it.

❼ Vannatter returns to the front of the house; dawn has broken. He sees drops of blood leading from the Bronco to the front door of the house. Soon, Arnelle picks up Simpson's youngest children from police custody. At about 7 a.m., Vannatter instructs officers to secure a search warrant for the residence, and the house is officially deemed a crime scene.

AP/Karl Tate, Wm. J. Castello, Eileen Glanton

January 11, 1995

Los Angeles (AP)

O. J. SIMPSON THREW HIS EX-WIFE out of a moving car, beat her during sex and threatened to cut off the heads of her boyfriends, according to entries from her diary and other explosive documents released by prosecutors Wednesday.

And in court, a prosecutor revealed that five days before Nicole Brown Simpson was killed she contacted a battered women's shelter, saying her ex-husband was stalking her. She also kept evidence of abuse in a safe-deposit box, the prosecutor said.

The documents were filed as part of a hearing on whether to let the jury listen to evidence of longstanding violence in Simpson's relationship with Ms. Simpson. They portray Simpson as fiercely jealous and filled with rage, and allege that 17 years of abuse and degradation ended in Ms. Simpson's murder.

The hearing continues Thursday, when prosecutors plan to present another incident of domestic violence they say they uncovered.

At Wednesday's session, capping a graphic recitation of domestic violence incidents dating to 1977, Deputy District Attorney Lydia Bodin said Ms. Simpson contacted the Sojourn Shelter on June 7.

"Nicole Brown Simpson went to that place because she was afraid, and she had reason to be afraid," Bodin said. "She felt she was being stalked . . . and she named the defendant as the person stalking her."

But defense attorney Johnnie Cochran Jr. said Ms. Simpson contacted the Sojourn Shelter but didn't go there in person, and that she only called to discuss reconciling with Simpson, not to seek protection from him.

Bodin also said that when prosecutors broke open Ms. Simpson's safe-deposit box they found pictures of her bruised face, letters of apology from Simpson, news articles reporting his 1989 admission of spousal abuse and her will.

"She literally created an accounting, an audit trail of acts of violence because she wanted people to know what was going on in her life," Bodin said.

Simpson's lawyers derided prosecutors' presentation as an unfair attempt to try Simpson's character.

Although past bad acts by a defendant often are barred from evidence, Bodin and Deputy District Attorney Scott Gordon argued Simpson's showed a pattern of violence leading to Ms. Simpson's death.

"This murder took 17 years to commit," Gordon said. "Those punches and slaps were the prelude to a homicide."

Defense attorney Gerald Uelmen argued that the June 12 stabbing deaths of Ms. Simpson and her friend Ronald Goldman have all the hallmarks of a drug-related slaying, including being "committed by stealth" and involving use of a knife.

"Where is there any similarity between a bedroom argument in which both parties had been drinking and the argument escalates into a

Denise Brown, Nicole Brown Simpson's sister, at the announcement of the founding of the Nicole Brown Simpson Charitable Foundation for Battered Women.

Photo Clark Jones

Michelle Sabole of Los Angeles holds a candle during a vigil outside Nicole Brown Simpson's house. The demonstrators shouted "Shame, shame," "100 percent killer" and "This is for Ron and Nicole."

Photo Chris Martinez

slapping incident, and the slashing of two people's throats on a sidewalk?" Uelmen asked.

During the presentation, Simpson's jurors, who were ordered sequestered before the arguments began, were safely tucked away at their undisclosed hotel.

The documents include entries from Ms. Simpson's diary and excerpts from letters from Simpson.

Among other things, the documents say Ms. Simpson's house keys were stolen from her home about two weeks before she and Goldman were slashed to death, and Simpson was carrying the keys when he was arrested five days later.

The documents also include a previously unreported statement from a person at Ms. Simpson's funeral who said Simpson uttered over her casket: "I'm sorry . . . I'm sorry . . . I loved you too much."

Prosecutors said police responded as many as nine times to domestic abuse calls from Ms. Simpson.

Ms. Simpson's diary quotes Simpson as calling his pregnant wife a "fat ass," demanding she get an abortion and once beating her while they had sex.

The papers also say that after a night of drinking in the summer of 1989, Simpson hit Ms. Simpson and threw her out of a moving car.

According to the documents, Ms. Simpson told her mother that her ex-husband was stalking her. Ms. Simpson was quoted as saying he "is following me again Mommy. I'm scared. I go to the gas station, he's there. I go to the Payless shoe store, and he's there. I'm driving and he's behind me." The date of the conversation was not disclosed.

Eddie Reynoza, who acted along with Simpson in the movie *Naked Gun 2½,* alleged in the court papers that Simpson once said if he ever caught Ms. Simpson's boyfriends driving his cars, he would "cut their (expletive) heads off!"

Simpson allegedly made the statement in 1991, while the two were still married. They divorced in 1992.

The alleged threat was the most dramatic statement yet suggesting a motive for the slayings. Goldman was allowed to drive Ms. Simpson's Ferrari, although friends and family said his relationship with Ms. Simpson was platonic.

Uelmen belittled Reynoza as an opportunist "advancing his own career by assigning himself a starring role in People vs. Simpson."

"What we ended up with is a bumpy marriage in which the parties argued a lot, probably no more than usual," Uelmen said in asking Judge Lance Ito to bar all evidence of violence in the Simpsons' relationship. "All the good moments of that marriage were left out."

In one letter, Simpson expressed regret for a New Year's 1989 fight that sent Ms. Simpson to the hospital and resulted in Simpson pleading no-contest to wife beating.

He wrote that he was "thinking and trying to realize how I got so crazy. . . . Nicole I love you

Nicole's sister, Denise Brown, testifies.

Photo Mark J. Terrill

more than ever as I watched you at the party. . . . It must be because of those feelings that I reacted so emotionally."

Simpson became agitated in court Wednesday when Uelmen brought up the 1989 fight. According to Uelmen, the Simpsons were drunk when they "got into an argument in their bedroom during which Mr. Simpson admitted he slapped and punched" his wife.

"I didn't do it. I didn't do it," Simpson was seen mouthing to another defense attorney.

Road through the U.S. legal system

Seven months after O.J. Simpson was charged with two counts of murder, his trial in Los Angeles Superior Court is set to begin. Here, the judicial twists and turns a criminal case can take:

Arrest
The suspect in a crime is placed in legal custody.

Simpson was arrested June 17.

Arraignment
The charge is read to the defendant, who then must enter a plea. Bond and a date for the preliminary hearing are set.

Simpson pleaded not guilty and was held without bail.

Grand jury hearing
Prosecution may opt to have a panel of citizens listen to charges and determine whether to indict the suspect. An indictment is a formal accusation.

Simpson's grand jury was dismissed when the judge determined the group had been unfairly influenced by massive publicity.

Preliminary hearing
A judge hears testimony to determine whether there is enough evidence to bring a defendant to trial. In low-profile cases, this stage is generally brief, with the prosecution presenting a bare-bones version of its case. However, the defense can cross-examine, as Simpson's lawyers did in Los Angeles.

Simpson's hearing was televised nationwide.

Arraignment
Defendant again enters a plea, and a trial date is set.

Simpson was arraigned in Superior Court July 22.

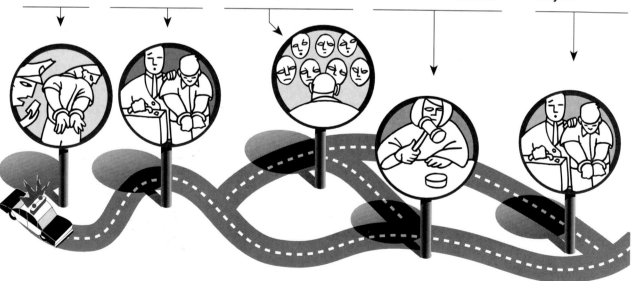

Pretrial motions

Lawyers argue the legality of evidence, fairness of the proceedings thus far, etc. As the trial date nears, a jury is selected. Judge Lance Ito has sequestered the jury to prevent the flow of outside information.

Trial

Prosecution and defense state what they intend to prove. Lawyers present all evidence for their sides, including documents, weapons, clothing and witnesses. Lawyers may attempt to have information thrown out or regarded as immaterial.

Mistrial

Declared if the judge believes the jury has heard improper evidence or the trial appears unfair in any way. Case thrown out.

Verdict

The jury deliberates the case. The jury must agree beyond a reasonable doubt that a defendant is guilty. If there is any uncertainty, they must acquit the defendant.

Sentencing

The judge sets the date and determines the penalty. **Simpson could face life imprisonment. Prosecutors decided not to call for the death penalty.**

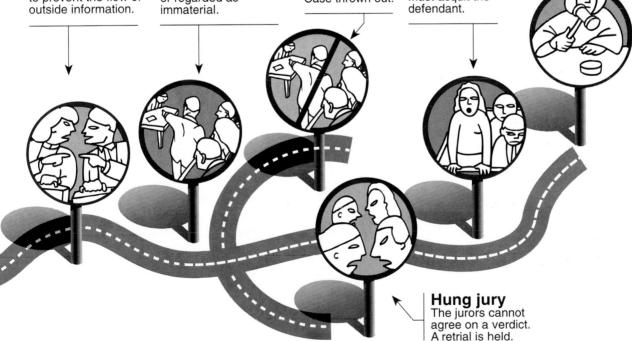

Hung jury

The jurors cannot agree on a verdict. A retrial is held.

Sources: American Bar Association, Randolph Stone; AP research

AP/Text: Eileen Glanton; Graphics: K. Gude; Research: Dawn Desilets

January 13, 1995

Los Angeles (AP)

TEMPERS FLARED as a black defense lawyer and black prosecutor excoriated each other for playing the race card—and using "the n-word"—in the O.J. Simpson trial.

Accusations flew. And then Simpson wept.

The sharp words and tears came Friday as prosecutors tried to stop defense lawyers from arguing that Detective Mark Fuhrman, a key witness, has a history of using racial epithets and expressing hatred for blacks and interracial couples.

Simpson confers with Carl Douglas, left front, and Cochran, partly hidden, after he waived his right to visit the Bundy Avenue murder scene.

Photo Tara Farrell

As both sides sparred over the issue of race, Deputy District Attorney Christopher Darden pleaded with the judge to prohibit defense lawyers from using the "the n-word."

"It is the dirtiest, filthiest, nastiest word in the English language," Darden said. "It'll upset the black jurors. It'll issue a test, and the test will be: 'Whose side are you on, the side of the white prosecutors and the white policemen, or are you on the side of the black defendant and his very prominent and capable black lawyer?' "

Defense lawyer Johnnie L. Cochran taunted Darden by reading from documents that quoted Fuhrman using the word "nigger." He called Darden's objections insulting to the eight blacks on the jury, which wasn't present for the hearing.

"African-Americans live with offensive words, offensive looks, offensive treatment every day of their lives," Cochran said. "And yet they still believe in this country."

Simpson is charged with murdering his ex-wife Nicole Brown Simpson and her friend Ronald Goldman. Simpson is black; both victims are white.

Impassive for most of the hearing, Simpson wiped tears from his eyes during an exchange between the two lawyers about his ex-wife.

Darden suggested that Simpson "has a fetish for blonde-haired white women," but said the prosecution wouldn't bring that up at trial because "that would inflame the passions of the jury."

Cochran berated Darden for such a suggestion, calling it "perhaps the most incredible remark I've heard in a court of law in the 32 years I've been practicing."

"How outrageous is this?" Cochran said. "If this man loves somebody who is purple, he has the right to get married. . . . His first wife was African-American. That's the beauty of America. That's what people have fought and died for."

Superior Court Judge Lance Ito was clearly disturbed by the bickering.

"This is the one main unresolved problem of our society," Ito said. "And for those of us who grew up in the sixties and had hoped this would kind of go away, it's a big disappointment to still have to read this stuff."

It was not immediately clear when Ito would rule. Opening statements are scheduled for Thursday.

Fuhrman is the detective who discovered a bloody glove at Simpson's estate the day after the killings. The glove matched one found at the crime scene.

Defense lawyers have tried since summer to brand Fuhrman a racist cop capable of planting the evidence to frame Simpson.

Fuhrman played a major role in Simpson's preliminary hearing, but prosecutors said Friday his trial testimony would be limited to his discovery of the bloody glove and his interview with Simpson's houseguest, Kato Kaelin.

Defense attorney Gerald Uelmen ridiculed what he said was the prosecution's thought of "scooting Detective Fuhrman in here for two minutes, have him testify about the glove and scoot him out. My reaction is—not in your dreams!"

Cochran read into the record several statements from Fuhrman, Fuhrman's psychologists and a woman who claimed she heard him make racist statements.

Kathleen Bell said in a sworn affidavit that Fuhrman told her: "If I had my way, they would take all the niggers, put them together in a big group and burn them." Fuhrman has denied ever meeting Bell.

February 3, 1995

Los Angeles (AP)

NICOLE BROWN SIMPSON'S SISTER burst into sobs on the witness stand Friday as she described how a raging O.J. Simpson threw his wife out of his house and once grabbed her crotch in a crowded bar, declaring: "This belongs to me."

Denise Brown, who has stated publicly she believes Simpson killed her sister, had just begun to recite a litany of violent and humiliating acts when she was overcome by tears, and the judge recessed court for the day.

The last thing the jurors heard before they returned to their hotel for the weekend was the sound of her sobs and her words, "It's just so hard."

Her testimony, the centerpiece of the prosecution's domestic violence accusations against Simpson, is to continue Monday.

Outside court, defense attorney Johnnie Cochran Jr. suggested the timing of her appearance was calculated for dramatic effect.

"I saw it coming, and we kept trying to say it's not fair," Cochran said.

Brown, questioned by Deputy District Attorney Christopher Darden and interrupted frequently by defense objections, told of two incidents from the 1980s—one in which Simpson grabbed his wife's crotch, and another when he hurled Ms. Simpson against a wall and threw her and others out of his mansion.

The defense objected repeatedly to Brown's injecting her opinions with such remarks as "he loved the attention" and "he has a big ego." The jurors were told to disregard such comments.

During a break in questioning,

Denise Brown in tears during some of her testimony.

Photo Mark J. Terrill

Simpson looked across the room at Brown and shook his head with a disgusted look. He appeared to try to catch her eye several times, but she stared straight ahead.

The 37-year-old Brown, who bears a striking resemblance to her younger sister, has become a spokeswoman for the family, telling her story on talk shows long before she testified.

She wore black on the witness stand, with a large cross around her neck and golden angel pins and earrings. The family has adopted angel jewelry as a symbol of Ms. Simpson.

She bit her lip and shifted in her chair as she testified.

Darden tried to start his narrative of the Simpsons' relationship with instances of abuse dating to 1977, when Simpson, still married to his first wife, invited Nicole, her sisters and some friends to see him play football for the Buffalo Bills in New York.

Brown said Simpson got upset at a post-game party and "started screaming at Nicole." The judge stopped the account, ruling it too remote in time to be relevant.

Instead, the story jumped ahead to 1985, when the Simpsons were married, and on to the late 1980s, when Brown recalled a gathering at a restaurant and bar with Simpson, his wife and assorted friends. The restaurant was crowded, and Simpson was instantly recognized and treated to drinks by admirers.

"We were all drinking and goofing around and being loud and dancing," Brown said. "At one point, O.J. grabbed Nicole's crotch and said, 'This is where babies come from and this belongs to me.' "

She said Ms. Simpson seemed used to such treatment.

"I thought it was humiliating," Brown said.

Another time, she said, she and her boyfriend dined with the Simpsons at a Mexican restaurant and ended up at Simpson's estate, where they were drinking at his bar.

"I told him he took Nicole for granted, and he blew up," Brown said.

"He started yelling—'Me? I don't take her for granted. I do everything for her. I give her everything,' " Brown said.

"And then a whole fight broke out. And pictures started flying off the walls. Clothes started flying. He ran upstairs, got clothes—started flying down the stairs, and um, grabbed Nicole, told her to get out of his house, wanted us all out of his house, picked her up, threw her against a wall," Brown said.

At that point, she choked out the rest of her description through tears: Simpson "picked (Nicole) up, threw her out of the house, she ended up on her—she ended up falling, she ended up on her elbows and on her butt. Then

February 3, 1995

Denise Brown was her dead sister's surrogate in the courtroom. If Nicole had been a brunette, she and Denise could have been twins. It was a resemblance that sent chills through the courtroom.

It was Denise who, along with her mother and sisters, began wearing angel pins to court in memory of the dead Nicole. Once, prosecutor Marcia Clark joined their demonstration, pinning an angel on her suit lapel. The defense complained and the judge ordered the lawyer to remove the pin.

When Ms. Brown took the stand, she wore a cross around her neck, an angel pin and angel earrings.

he threw Ed McCabe out. We were all sitting there screaming and crying and he grabbed me and threw me out of the house."

Jurors were riveted by the testimony, and some looked over at Simpson as the witness spoke. They watched as Deputy District Attorney Marcia Clark placed an arm around Brown and escorted her from the witness stand.

Simpson is charged in the June 12 slashing murders of Ms. Simpson and her friend Ronald Goldman. Prosecutors are seeking to show he was an obsessed, jealous man who abused his wife during their marriage, stalked her after they split and killed her in a rage.

Earlier Friday, two of Ms. Simpson's former next-door neighbors said that Simpson once parked around the corner from her house late at night and stood outside, seemingly trying to peer into the window. They called the police.

"I didn't recognize him. I said to myself, what is a man of this description doing outside at this time?" Carl Colby said of his 911 call in April 1992, months after Ms. Simpson had moved out on her husband.

But moments after Colby called police, he got a closer look and realized it was Simpson, who frequently visited his children at his wife's house.

"I was embarrassed that I'd called 911 because I didn't feel Mr. Simpson was a threat to me or anyone else in the neighborhood," Colby said.

Colby said that Simpson "seemed to be hesitant and to be attempting to perhaps observe something that may have been occurring inside the house." But he said Simpson never stepped onto the property.

Colby's wife, Catherine Boe, testified that Simpson had parked around the corner instead of at the curb or in Ms. Simpson's wide driveway.

In cross-examining the couple, defense attorney Robert Shapiro offered an innocent explanation for Simpson's presence that night, suggesting the former football star might have a meeting arranged with his estranged wife.

And Shapiro suggested that Simpson parked around the corner rather than leave the car under a tree that might drop sticky debris on it.

February 8, 1995

Los Angeles (AP)

PROSECUTORS IN THE O.J. SIMPSON CASE Wednesday tried to fix the time of the murders by way of a "Mary Tyler Moore Show" rerun and the howls of an agitated dog found wandering the neighborhood with blood on its paws.

The dog, identified as Nicole Brown Simpson's Akita, ultimately led a neighbor to Ms. Simpson's body in the blood-spattered brick walkway of her condo.

The neighbor, Sukru Boztepe, testified that he took the dog for a walk to calm it down, and recalled how the animal was "getting more nervous and it was pulling me harder." Around midnight, he said, the dog stopped at Ms. Simpson's home and looked down the dark walkway. Boztepe's eyes followed.

"I saw a lady laying down, full of blood," Boztepe told the jury. "She was blonde. I could see her arm."

Boztepe said he and his wife, who was with him that night, alerted neighbors to call police. They didn't see the body of Ronald Goldman.

With no known witnesses to the crime and a coroner unable to fix the time of death, prosecutors are seeking to convince jurors that the barking of Ms. Simpson's dog, named Kato, can establish to within minutes when she and Goldman were slashed to death the night of June 12.

Under questioning from prosecutor Marcia Clark, Eva Stein, one of several neighbors called to the stand, said "very loud, very persistent" barking woke her up around 10:15 P.M. and kept her from falling back to sleep.

On Tuesday, another neighbor, screenwriter Pablo Fenjves, likewise said he heard the "plaintive wails" of a dog about 10:15 or 10:20 P.M.

Ms. Stein's live-in boyfriend, Louis Karpf, testified Wednesday that he arrived home from a trip about 10:45 or 10:50 P.M., went out to get the mail and "saw a dog in the street coming at me, barking very profusely. . . . It started to approach me, which did scare me, so I actually retreated back inside my gate until it moved on."

Then there was Steven Schwab, a neighbor whose nightly dog-walking routine was dictated by when his favorite TV reruns came on. It was Sunday, and he recalled taking his dog out at the end of "The Dick Van Dyke Show" at 10:30 P.M.

During his walk, he said, he checked his watch. It was 10:55 when he saw a dog on the loose outside a condo.

As he approached the white-and-tan animal, he said, he noticed blood on its paws and thought it might be hurt. As he headed home, he said, the dog followed, and "would howl at every house we passed. It would stop and bark down the path."

Later, he said, he examined the Akita and found no injuries that would account for the moist blood. He turned the dog over to Boztepe.

The hour in question

9:10 p.m.
Simpson drives houseguest Brian "Kato" Kaelin to McDonald's in his Bentley.

9:36 p.m.
Simpson and Kaelin return to Simpson's estate on Rockingham Avenue.

10:03 p.m.
Simpson telephones his girlfriend, Paula Barbieri, from the cellular phone in his Bronco.

10:15 p.m.
Nicole Simpson's neighbor Pablo Fenjves hears a dog barking, then a "plaintive wail."

10:22 p.m.
Limousine driver Allan Park drives down Rockingham and doesn't see Bronco.

10:40 p.m.
Park pulls up to the gate on Ashford Street and rings the buzzer. Nobody answers.

10:45-50 p.m.
Ms. Simpson's neighbor sees Ms. Simpson's Akita, with bloody paws, on the sidewalk outside her house.

10:51-52 p.m.
Kaelin hears three thumps on the wall outside his guest house.

10:54 p.m.
Park sees a man he believes is Simpson entering the front door at Rockingham.

11:15 p.m.
Simpson and Park leave for the airport.

AP

February 8, 1995

In a case heavy with scientific evidence, small heart-tugging details were the most memorable. The story of Kato the dog touched animal lovers worldwide, and brought an outpouring of inquiries about the pup. Many said if Kato could speak, the murder mystery would have been solved. The tan-and-white Akita, his paws soaked in blood, wandered the Brentwood neighborhood trying to summon help for his mistress, Nicole Brown Simpson.

The dog's odyssey also uncovered a Brentwood subculture—the dog walkers. Never have so many witnesses come forward with information gleaned while they were out walking their dogs. Their testimony also offered insight into lifestyles on the trendy west side of Los Angeles where neighbors such as Steven Schwab set their watches by the TV sitcom reruns they watched religiously. His favorites were "Mary Tyler Moore" and "Dick Van Dyke."

A dog, believed to be the Akita named "Kato" owned by Nicole Brown Simpson, stands by the gate of O.J. Simpson's home. Police believed the persistent barking of "Kato" alerted neighbors to the murders of Simpson and Goldman.

Photo Chris Pizzello

On cross-examination, defense attorney Johnnie Cochran Jr. tried to show that witnesses were only approximating the times that they heard the dog. Some acknowledged that might be the case. But not Schwab.

When he returned home, he said, his wife was watching TV and it was precisely 11:05 P.M. "The Mary Tyler Moore Show" had just begun; it was the episode in which Mary was dating someone from a competing TV station, he said.

The timing of the crime is critical: Prosecutors allege Simpson killed his ex-wife and Goldman at 10:15 P.M., allowing himself enough time to return to his estate, clean up and get into a limousine for the airport at about 11 P.M.

In opening statements, Cochran ridiculed the prosecution's effort to convict Simpson based on a dog's howl. He said the former football star was practicing his golf swing in his yard at the time of the slayings.

During his testimony, Schwab's route that night was outlined for jurors on a multicolor electronic map, much the way plays are outlined by commentators during football games.

Both Karpf and Schwab were shown a photo of Ms. Simpson's Akita and identified it as the dog they had seen.

February 12, 1995

Los Angeles (AP)

As O.J. SIMPSON SAT in a police car a block away, jurors toured the murder scene Sunday and took copious notes at the spot where the slashed, crumpled bodies of his ex-wife and her friend were found in pools of blood.

Simpson later visited his estate for the first time since his June 17 arrest. With a few plainclothes deputies nearby, he stood in the front yard of his Brentwood mansion chatting with lawyers for about two hours as jurors toured his property.

Simpson's house on Rockingham Drive.

Photo Mark J. Terrill

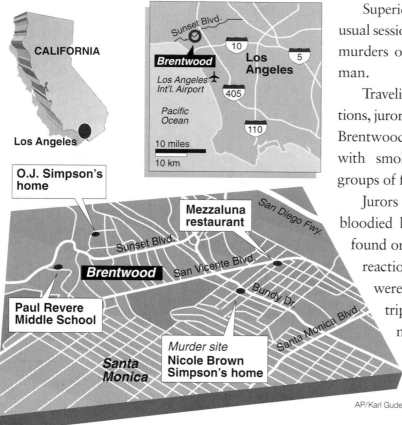

CALIFORNIA

Los Angeles

Sunset Blvd.
Brentwood
Los Angeles
Int'l. Airport
Pacific
Ocean
10 10 miles
405 10 km
Los Angeles
5
110

O.J. Simpson's home

Mezzaluna restaurant

San Diego Fwy.

Sunset Blvd.

Brentwood
San Vicente Blvd.

Paul Revere Middle School

Bundy Dr.

Santa Monica Blvd.

Murder site
Nicole Brown Simpson's home

Santa Monica

AP/Karl Gude

Superior Court Judge Lance Ito convened an unusual session for the tour eight months to the day after the murders of Nicole Brown Simpson and Ronald Goldman.

Traveling in a motorcade of presidential proportions, jurors stopped at the murder scene at Ms. Simpson's Brentwood condominium. They stepped out of their bus with smoked-glass windows and were escorted in groups of four in and around the house.

Jurors took notes of their observations where the bloodied bodies of Ms. Simpson and Goldman were found on the walkway leading up to the house. Their reactions inside weren't known because reporters were barred from the house. Prosecutors said the trip allowed jurors to see that the walkway is narrow and confined.

"It would (show) the reason why one person could accomplish this, and how the victims were cornered," Deputy District Attorney Marcia Clark said.

February 12, 1995

We packed sandwiches and cell phones, put on our most comfortable walking shoes and prepared for duty. We were the pool reporters assigned to the jury's field trip to O.J. Simpson's estate and the scene of his ex-wife's murder. Our mission: to phone every detail to our colleagues downtown awaiting word on the caravan, on the

Continued on following page

BRENTWOOD
Sunset Blvd.
Rockingham Ave.
40
O.J. Simpson's estate
Ashford St.
Nicole Simpson's home
San Vicente Blvd.
26th St.
Montana Ave.
Wilshire Blvd.
Bundy Dr.
.5 mile
.5 km
SANTA MONICA

Grounds of O.J. Simpson's home

Evidence seized by police included blood found on the driveway and in the white Ford Bronco. A bloody glove was also found on the premises.

ROCKINGHAM AVE.
ASHFORD ST.
Wall
Lawn
Tennis court
Simpson's white Bronco
Play area
Entrance
Family room
Pool
Brian "Kato" Kaelin's room
Driveway
Garage
Fence

AP/Karl Tate

The crime scene.

Photo Eric Draper

Defense lawyer Johnnie Cochran Jr. disagreed.

"How do you have a life-and-death fight in an area that small and not have bruises?" Cochran asked. "The jurors had to be amazed at that."

Later, on the last stop of the six-hour tour, Simpson appeared relaxed and happy at his house. As he stood amid the greenery and flowers, he appeared to be showing points of interest to the deputies guarding him.

But after he had gone inside the house for about 10 minutes and strolled around the property with his lawyers, his brow was furrowed and he appeared drained.

Jurors were escorted through Simpson's bedroom, bathroom, closet, kitchen, garage, laundry room and trophy room. They also poked into the room used by former Simpson guest Brian "Kato" Kaelin, a witness in the trial. Prosecutors complained about fresh flowers around the house and two fireplaces burning, Cochran said. The judge allowed them, but ordered that a picture of Simpson's mother be removed from his bedside table after determining that it hadn't always been there, Cochran said.

Prosecutors also said a Bible was displayed on a table in the house. As in court, Simpson wasn't handcuffed or shackled. He also wasn't wearing an

Continued from previous page

jury's reactions and on Simpson's return to his beloved home.

It was a day stored in memory snapshots: the motorcade wending past murder landmarks on streets lined with spectators; families with children and pets pausing in their Sunday morning strolls to watch history unfold. The jurors, amateur Sherlock Holmes types, examining every blade of grass, every inch of sidewalk and writing down notes to themselves.

And there was Simpson, lord of the manor, returning to his domain as a prisoner but falling quickly into the role of host to his retinue of guards and court personnel. He stood on the lawn in the warm afternoon sunshine gesturing around his property, showing his guests the spread. When it was over, he appeared drained. His jail cell awaited. Would he ever come home again? No one was sure. As the vans pulled away, Simpson's last view was his maid, Gigi, closing the gate, smiling wistfully and waving good-bye.

F. Lee Bailey joined the defense team before the trial began.

Photo Reed Saxon

raucous laughter from just about everyone in the courtroom, including Simpson and jurors.

But Kaelin, who became an instant celebrity last summer after testifying at Simpson's preliminary hearing, also began relating a story central to Simpson's fate.

He told how he came to live with the former football star, spoke of Simpson's broken marriage and new romance, and recalled Simpson's plans for June 12, 1994, the day Nicole Brown Simpson and Ronald Goldman were slashed to death.

The court day ended before Kaelin could describe the thumps in the night that led police to a bloody glove, a key piece of evidence in the murder case against Simpson.

The witness, his unkempt blond hair now below his shoulders, made his entrance after Detective Philip Vannatter ended three days on the witness stand by acknowledging misstatements and questionable handling of evidence.

Court transcripts also confirm for the first time that the "mystery envelope," which surfaced last summer, contains a knife that was not the murder weapon. Despite a request by the defense, the judge barred jurors from seeing the knife, for now.

Kaelin, a much-anticipated witness, appeared nervous. He virtually ran into the courtroom, then had to leave when lawyers weren't ready for him. Moments later, when he raced back in, several jurors smiled at him, as did Simpson and spectators in the crowded courtroom.

Many of the jurors appeared tickled to see Kaelin up close. One female juror appeared on the verge of laughter throughout his testimony.

When Kaelin was asked to point out Simpson in the courtroom, the defendant smiled and gave a little wave to his former tenant.

"A bit nervous today?" Deputy District Attorney Marcia Clark asked the fidgeting witness when he first took the stand.

"Feel great," Kaelin replied, then quickly added, "a little nervous."

Kaelin, often squinting, shifting in his chair and licking his lips, told jurors he met Nicole Brown Simpson in December 1992 in Aspen, Colorado. He said they became friends and he moved into her guest house a month later, sometimes caring for her two children to defray the monthly rent of about $500.

He moved into Simpson's guest quarters, rent-free, in January 1994, when Ms. Simpson moved to another condominium that had no separate guest house.

Clark asked Kaelin if he thought his relationship with Simpson would help his acting career.

"I didn't think that. I just never asked," Kaelin replied. "I was getting things on my own . . ."

Marcia Clark.

Photo Lois Bernstein

He paused, then delivered the uproarious punch line about the improbability of competing for movie roles with one of America's best-known celebrities.

After identifying photographs of his room at Simpson's house and explaining the living arrangement, Kaelin was asked what he knew of Simpson's feelings for his ex-wife.

"Their relationship was over," he said.

"He told you they were broken up for good?" Clark asked.

"Yes," Kaelin said.

On the night of the murders, he said, Simpson had plans to attend his daughter Sydney's dance recital and didn't want his new girlfriend, Paula Barbieri, to come along.

"Paula wanted to go," Kaelin said, adding, "I think O.J. wanted to make it kind of a family thing, just be on his own."

"Did he tell you Paula was upset because she wanted to go to the recital?" Clark asked.

"Yes," Kaelin said.

"She wanted to show Nicole she was the defendant's girl?" Clark asked.

The question drew an angry response from Simpson, who shook his head vehemently and commented to his attorneys. The judge sustained an objection to the question, and it went unanswered.

March 27, 1995

Los Angeles (AP)

THERE IS BLOOD EVERYWHERE. Pools of it on the ground around the slashed, crumpled bodies of Nicole Brown Simpson and Ronald Goldman. A red river dripping down the steps from her condominium and tracked by someone's shoes through a back corridor.

Pictures of this grisly crime scene, barred from television, repeatedly have been projected onto a seven-foot screen for jurors.

Now, prosecutors want to blow up autopsy pictures, a proposal that raises anew the question of how such horror shows affect jurors in the murder trial of O.J. Simpson.

Prosecutors say this jury is up to the task.

"The jurors and alternates were extensively (questioned) on their ability to view graphic or gruesome photos without becoming upset or losing their ability to be fair and impartial," prosecutors said in a motion last week seeking to show the autopsy photos.

In fact, they said, the photos are less gruesome than those already seen by the jury because the blood has been cleaned up.

Legal experts say the photos will most likely be admitted but they are divided on whether Superior Court Judge Lance Ito will—or should—let them be flashed on the huge courtroom screen.

"Technology raises its own issues," Loyola University law professor Laurie Levenson said. "I think Judge Ito will put them on the large screen because he wants to make them available and visible."

Levenson notes that a jury inundated with gruesome crime scene photos may be immune to the impact of autopsy photos.

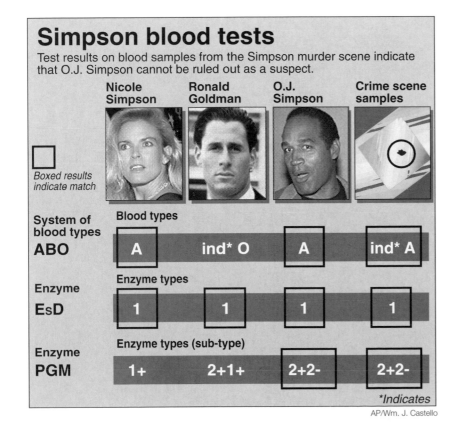

Simpson blood tests

Test results on blood samples from the Simpson murder scene indicate that O.J. Simpson cannot be ruled out as a suspect.

	Nicole Simpson	Ronald Goldman	O.J. Simpson	Crime scene samples
Boxed results indicate match				
System of blood types **ABO** — Blood types	A	ind* O	A	ind* A
Enzyme **EsD** — Enzyme types	1	1	1	1
Enzyme **PGM** — Enzyme types (sub-type)	1+	2+1+	2+2-	2+2-

*Indicates

AP/Wm. J. Castello

March 27, 1995

Perhaps the most important witness in the Simpson trial was Elmo. That was the name of the high-tech computerized show-and-tell system that allowed pictures to be projected on a giant screen where lawyers could use electronic pointers and other gadgetry to highlight points of testimony.

"Do you see the spot of blood?" a lawyer would ask, then pull a colored arrow from the air to highlight the picture on the screen. Witnesses could use electronic colored pencils to draw circles around important locations and sign their initials. Scientific experts used the system to illustrate their complex lectures on DNA.

Most affecting were huge photos of the slain Nicole Brown Simpson and Ronald Goldman projected on the screen in vivid color. Simpson would often catch his breath and look away when those photos were shown, and the judge would cut the video feed. Viewers saw the entire trial, but the gruesome photographs were ruled off-limits for public consumption.

UCLA law professor Peter Arenella said Ito could "use the wisdom of Solomon and say in this case we will use smaller pictures and pass them around to the jurors."

While defense attorneys often object to the use of autopsy and crime scene photos, Arenella said courts almost always admit them if there is a rationale.

Simpson's prosecutors said they want to answer defense claims that more than one person committed the murders. The defense has not yet filed its response to the prosecution motion.

Arenella suggested the prosecution motives may be more subtle.

"In a trial in which the victims are gone but the defendant is in front of the jury every day, it's easier for the jury to relate to his humanity," Arenella said. "The prosecution wants a constant reminder of the victims' humanity and the pictures provide that."

Or, as Southwestern University Professor Robert Pugsley explained it, "This is the way to bring back the bodies from 6 feet underground, thrust them in the face of the jury and say, 'That's why we're here.'"

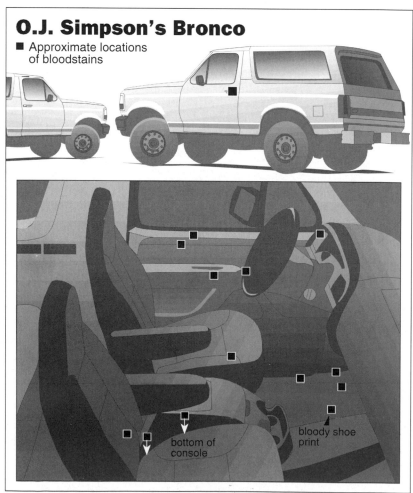

O.J. Simpson's Bronco
■ Approximate locations of bloodstains

bottom of console

bloody shoe print

Source: Los Angeles Police Dept.   AP/Karl Gude

April 21, 1995

Los Angeles (AP)

JUROR TENSIONS IN THE O.J. SIMPSON TRIAL erupted into open revolt today when 13 panelists protested the replacement of sheriff's guards and demanded a meeting with the judge, sources said.

Some of the jurors were seen crying as they were taken back to their hotel after court Thursday afternoon, a source said.

The resumption of testimony by a police criminalist was canceled today as Superior Court Judge Lance Ito scrambled to resolve the turmoil in the sequestered jury.

Ito met with lawyers and sheriff's officials behind closed doors. And he

Jury Revolt Day

It began with whispers. A bailiff said it first. Then it spread among the reporters. A jury rebellion was under way. Details were hard to come by. Some said the sequestered panelists had refused to leave their hotel; others said they had been seen crying.

"They're all wearing black," a deputy reported. It sounded ominous. Testimony was suspended and an inquiry began. It turned out that the jurors were upset because three of their guards had been removed from the jury detail. But the uprising was symptomatic of general jury unrest, and one woman seized the opportunity to demand that she be released, weeping, "I can't take it anymore."

By trial's end, 10 of the first 24 jurors chosen had been dismissed; rumors of discord were rampant and most observers were betting on a hung jury. Then the jury surprised everyone by reaching the quickest verdict in memory.

During the trial.

Photo Douglas C. Pizac

Cochran and Clark often clashed.

Photo Kevork Djansezian

met individually with jurors who asked to speak to him, said court spokeswoman Jerrianne Hayslett. Attorneys from both sides and a Sheriff's Department official, Cmdr. Patrick Holland, sat in on the meetings, which were recorded by a court reporter, she said.

Ito talked to seven jurors today and planned to talk to others on Monday, Hayslett said.

"He is probably considering this part of his ongoing inquiry," she said.

The resumption of testimony by criminalist Andrea Mazzola was put off until Tuesday.

Sheriff Sherman Block resumed a public defense of his deputies today, saying the judge acted precipitously in removing the three. "I hate to be an I-told-you-so kind of thing, but I think had he completed this investigation he might not have the turmoil that he has this morning," he added.

Legal analyst Myrna Raeder, a law professor at Southwestern University, said it was too early

Arnelle Simpson and Al Cowlings bring flowers to Nicole Brown Simpson's grave site on Friday, May 19, 1995, on what would have been Nicole's 36th birthday.

Photo Chris Pizzello

to speculate on what action Ito must take. She said the judge needed to worry about emotional issues before legal issues, interviewing the jurors and getting to the bottom of the dispute.

"Ito has got to be very sensitive in making sure that he puts this back together again without the requirement of a mistrial," said Raeder.

The rebellious panelists asked to speak to Ito at their hotel this morning before the court session, but the judge said they had to come to court to speak with him, sheriff's sources said.

The jury then was driven to the courthouse, arriving about 9 A.M. Thirteen were dressed completely or partially in black. At noon they left, stone-faced, to return to their hotel.

The court did not announce a reason for the juror uprising. But the action came a day after Ito ordered the removal of three deputies, apparently in response to complaints by a dismissed juror that some white members of the panel got preferential treatment.

The judge's decision angered Block, who said the judge didn't even interview the deputies involved.

"I just think it is wholly inappropriate to take the action that he did relative to these deputies," Block said, adding that the slow pace of the trial was to blame for juror discontent.

"I have every confidence that the deputies performed their duties professionally and consistent with their responsibility," he said.

Besides the deputies' dismissals, the trial was shaken by another possible jury problem Thursday, which overshadowed the start of testimony by Mazzola, the rookie technician who collected most of the evidence in the case.

In a private meeting with the judge, juror No. 453, a 25-year-old black flight attendant, asked to be released from jury duty. "I can't take it anymore," she said, according to a transcript. Ito took no immediate action.

Southwestern University law professor Robert Pugsley said it was unlikely Ito would dismiss the juror without further investigation. Pugsley said the judge should release her only if there were evidence of misconduct, a medical reason or some emergency.

"I think that Judge Ito would be well-advised not to let her off because it would set a very dangerous precedent," Pugsley said. "There's any number of jurors and alternates . . . who have equally good reasons and are equally fed up with being on this jury."

Professor Raeder said Ito made "an excellent decision" to dismiss the deputies, even if the deputies didn't do anything wrong.

"It really seems to me if enough individuals have a perception that the deputies were exacerbating . . . racial tension, then they should be removed, because the comfort of the jury panel as a whole is what we have to ensure," Raeder said.

June 15, 1995

Los Angeles (AP)

WITH JURORS WATCHING WIDE-EYED, O.J. Simpson struggled Thursday to shove his hands into the bloody leather gloves that prosecutors say implicate him in two murders. "They're too small," the defendant declared.

The demonstration provided perhaps the most dramatic moment in Simpson's trial and appeared to backfire on the prosecutor who requested it.

Simpson grimaced and raised his eyebrows as he tried to pull the distinctive Aris Leather Light gloves

O.J. Simpson gloves

An expert testified today he was "100 percent certain" the gloves O.J. Simpson wore during a 1991 football broadcast were the same unique style as those found by murder investigators.

About the gloves:
■ Distinguished by their stitching
■ A V-shaped vent in the palm
■ A special hem at the wrist
■ Thin leather and lining

AP

Simpson and attorneys Cochran, Blasier and Neufeld during closing arguments.

Photo Reed Saxon

Clark shows Los Angeles Police Detective Tom Lange a stocking cap found at Nicole Brown Simpson's residence. Lange was one of the lead homicide detectives investigating the murders.

Photo Kevork Djansezian

over a pair of latex gloves he had to wear to protect the evidence. Even the stretchy latex gloves seemed to give the former football star problems.

Deputy District Attorney Christopher Darden tried to suggest to jurors that Simpson, an actor, was faking his struggle. Once Simpson had the gloves on as far as they could go, the prosecutor asked that he grip an object, a marking pen, to show he could bend his hand.

Simpson obliged over objections from defense attorney Johnnie Cochran Jr., grasping the marker in his right fist and holding it up for jurors. That glove is stained with blood that matches his, his ex-wife's and her friend's, prosecution experts have testified.

Richard Rubin, former vice president and general manager of Aris Isotoner Inc., which made the gloves for Bloomingdale's department stores, was asked by Darden to measure Simpson's hands.

The witness walked over to the defense table, held his own smaller hands up to Simpson's, eyeballed the spread of Simpson's knuckles then declared Simpson a size large or extra-large.

The gloves, one found at the murder scene, the mate found at Simpson's estate, are extra-large.

The prosecution's murder theory

1 The assailant stabs Nicole Simpson four times in the neck. At about the same time, she also has her head smashed against a gate or metal post.

2 The killer restrains Ronald Goldman with his left hand and carefully makes parallel cuts across his neck. Later, the assailant stabs Goldman behind the left ear and in the heart and lung.

3 With Goldman dead or dying, the attacker returns to Ms. Simpson, who may be unconscious, and pulls back her head by her hair. He slashes her throat with a knife in his right hand, killing her almost instantly.

4 The killer runs away up the steps to the back alley of Ms. Simpson's condo.

AP/Karl Gude

"At one point in time, those gloves would actually be, I think, large on Mr. Simpson's hands," Rubin told jurors. He suggested their age might have something to do with the fit.

Prosecutors tried to show that Nicole Brown Simpson unwittingly outfitted her ex-husband for her own murder by purchasing the gloves on a visit to New York.

When Darden won permission for Simpson to try on the gloves, jurors leaned forward as Simpson approached. They followed his hands with their eyes, and one juror appeared to breathe harder. When Simpson turned to return to his seat, several panelists began writing in their notebooks.

On his way across the courtroom, Simpson handed the leather gloves to Darden and

shrugged to his sisters in the audience. They exchanged smiles.

He then peeled off the latex gloves with snaps that resounded in the quiet courtroom, wadded them up and tossed them on the table.

"I think it was a very, very important day for us," Cochran said outside court. "He just couldn't get them on. There are no two ways about it."

But Darden countered, "We looked at his hands, we looked at the gloves. And even in their present condition, they should fit and do fit."

Loyola University law professor Laurie Levenson said it was "the worst night the prosecution has had in a long time. It should have been a golden moment and it backfired."

She said the prosecution broke a cardinal rule of courtroom law: "Don't do a demonstration in front of the jury unless you know how it's going to turn out."

Cochran challenged identification of the bloody gloves by a Bloomingdale's buyer, suggesting that a credit card receipt Ms. Simpson signed December 18, 1990, had nothing to do with the gloves in evidence.

Brenda Vemich testified that the gloves placed before her on the witness stand were Aris Leather Lights and designed exclusively for the department store. She cited the gloves' light leather, special stitching, cashmere lining and palm-side vent as distinguishing characteristics.

Vemich said that of the overall purchase of some 12,000 pairs of Leather Lights from Aris Isotoner, 300 were brown, size extra-large. Of those, she estimated 200 likely were sold.

The glove testimony followed the conclusion of a nine-day endurance run on the witness stand by the county coroner. Defense attorney Robert

Shapiro dramatized his cross-examination of Dr. Lakshmanan Sathyavagiswaran at one point by turning and twisting a knife to demonstrate the many angles at which it could stab or slash.

Shapiro wanted to show that a left-handed person could have killed Ms. Simpson and friend Ronald Goldman and that more than one killer could have been involved.

The coroner acknowledged he couldn't be "certain" whether the killer was right- or left-handed but quickly added, "The last wound on Nicole Brown Simpson had to be a right-handed person." Simpson is right-handed.

The cross-examination was relatively brief—about four hours—because the prosecution had pre-empted much of the defense attack on Sathyavagiswaran's office. Nevertheless, Shapiro managed to raise significant questions, the kind "that go straight to the heart of reasonable doubt," said Professor Robert Pugsley of Southwestern University School of Law.

Among those questions, Pugsley said, were: Was it just one killer? If one, was he or she right- or left-handed? Was it just one weapon? How would an athletic person like Goldman not give more resistance?

Los Angeles County coroner Dr. Lakshmanan Sathyavagiswaran demonstrates on prosecutor Brian Kelberg how Goldman's throat may have been slashed.

Photo Kevork Djansezian

Marcia Clark confers with the
prosecution during closing arguments.
AP Photo

July 6, 1995

Los Angeles (AP)

AFTER FIVE MONTHS OF LEGAL THEATRICS before a troubled jury and a transfixed nation, the prosecution finished its case against O.J. Simpson with one final glimpse of grisly autopsy photos and three simple words Thursday: "The people rest."

Now, a jury that already has lost 10 members of the original pool of 24 jurors and alternates will hear the defense, but not necessarily from Simpson himself.

That starts Monday, and the trial that has so far seen 58 witnesses and 488 exhibits could end before Labor Day.

"At this time, subject to receipt of the people's exhibits into evidence, the people rest," prosecutor Marcia Clark told Judge Lance Ito, ending a no-holds-barred effort to convict a beloved football hero in the stabbing deaths of his ex-wife Nicole Brown Simpson and her friend Ronald Goldman.

At least one trial watcher saw the ending as lacking punch.

"It had the sense to me of fatigue and a glad-to-be-over-with ending," Southwestern University law professor Robert Pugsley said. "It was sort of a low-key way to end such a lengthy, mountainous pile of evidence."

Of the overall presentation, he said: "I would call it a very credible case. I wouldn't call it a compelling case."

Jurors were excused until Monday, but attorneys were told to return Friday for a hearing on the admissibility of evidence.

As the trial progressed, viewers became as familiar with Shapiro and Cochran as they were with Simpson.

Photo Reed Saxon

Defense attorney Johnnie Cochran Jr. said the defense would decide overnight whether to file a motion for directed verdict of acquittal on the basis of insufficient evidence.

The prosecution built its case on blood and fibers and the mournful wailings of a barking dog, but in the end still had no eyewitness, no murder weapon and no definite motive.

Simpson maintained his calm but bit his lip as Clark displayed once again the pictures that were part of a gruesome display that sent two jurors fleeing from the courtroom earlier in the trial.

Cochran, and Simpson himself, made it clear outside the jury's presence they would put on witnesses. The defendant acknowledged he had been told that he could rest on the evidence and present nothing, but he had rejected that option.

Asked by Ito if he understood his legal rights, Simpson replied: "That is correct."

After 92 days of testimony and circumstantial evidence designed to portray Simpson as a jealous wife-abuser driven to murder, the defense was expected to begin resurrecting his image as a charismatic national celebrity, with testimony

The defendant.

Photo Lois Bernstein

from family members, golfing buddies and other friends.

Just before resting, the prosecution changed its mind by dropping plans to call Ms. Simpson's mother, Juditha Brown, as its final witness. Instead, a summary of what she would have told the jury was read into the record.

The statement recounted Mrs. Brown's last dinner with her daughter and a search for lost eyeglasses that, in a twist of fate, led Goldman to Ms. Simpson's condominium—and to his death.

Goldman, a waiter at the restaurant where the family had dined that night, was returning the glasses when the killer attacked.

Cochran objected to Clark's display of the photos at the end of her case, but the judge ruled

them relevant and allowed them to be flashed in front of jurors for five seconds.

The last witness for the prosecution was FBI hair and fiber expert Douglas Deedrick, who told jurors about the slender but strong hair and fiber evidence collected in the case.

Deedrick spent much of the morning undergoing a low-key cross-examination by F. Lee Bailey.

Opting for a gentle, respectful tone in cross-examination, Bailey followed the defense course of raising reasonable doubt about the origin of the prosecution's most incriminating evidence. Deedrick had told jurors that a hair similar to Simpson's was found on Goldman's shirt and rose-beige carpet fibers consistent with those from Simpson's Bronco were found scattered on

The prosecution rests

After five months and nearly five dozen witnesses, O.J. Simpson's prosecutors ended their case. A look at their successes and stumbles:

MISSES

HITS

The gloves

At the request of prosecutor Christopher Darden, Simpson struggled to put on the infamous bloody gloves, then told jurors, "They're too small."

The emotion

Early in the case, Nicole Brown Simpson's sister Denise wept on the witness stand as she detailed her sister's stormy relationship with O.J. Simpson. Months later, jurors viewed ghastly autopsy photos.

The criminalists

Evidence collectors Dennis Fung and Andrea Mazzola were shredded in cross-examination, allowing the defense to build two theories: That police used Simpson's blood sample to frame him, and that shoddy collection made the evidence useless.

Physical evidence

Prosecutors made a gradual, steady presentation of evidence, from the first bloody glove in February to clothing and carpet fibers discussed this week.

Brian "Kato" Kaelin

Marcia Clark first relied on the Simpson houseguest to help build a timeline for the night of the murders. But she later turned on him, suggesting he was protecting O.J. Simpson and declaring him a hostile witness.

The DNA

Scientist Robin Cotton offered a detailed explanation, then startling odds. The chances of matching characteristics in a blood drop at the murder scene and blood from a black or white person other than Simpson are less than 1 in 170 million.

The bag and shovel

Late one Friday, Detective Mark Fuhrman unwrapped a long-handled shovel and a large plastic bag. Both were found in Simpson's Bronco. The following Monday, prosecutors acknowledged the bag is standard Bronco equipment.

AP/Karl Gude, Eileen Glanton

crucial evidence. He also identified mysterious blue-black fibers, which prosecutors say came from Simpson's clothing.

Prosecutors alleged the evidence was left during a life-and-death struggle. Bailey posed alternate theories for how the hair and fiber evidence was deposited.

"If Mr. Goldman's body was dragged over soil and Mr. Simpson's hair was in that soil could there have been a transfer?" Bailey asked.

"Yes," Deedrick replied.

The defense has claimed that Simpson's hair is poor evidence because he paid frequent visits to his ex-wife's condominium and probably left traces of hair.

Clark asked Deedrick if the hair found on Goldman's shirt showed any signs of dirt; he said it did not. As for the blue-black fibers emphasized by the prosecution, Bailey elicited from Deedrick the fact that 5 billion pounds of cotton fiber was manufactured in the United States each year. The witness had no idea how much of it was blue-black.

Prosecutors suggested a link between the fibers and testimony that Simpson wore a dark sweat suit on the night of the murders.

July 10, 1995

Los Angeles (AP)

OJ. SIMPSON BEAMED AT HIS DAUGHTER and mother as they opened his defense Monday, telling jurors he was distressed after his ex-wife's murder and depicting as a drunk a friend who testified against him.

Simpson's daughter Arnelle, sister Carmelita Simpson-Durio and mother, Eunice, recalled a sometimes tearful Simpson, who was confused and upset the day the bodies of Nicole Brown Simpson and Ronald Goldman were found.

In a moment of high drama, Simpson's 73-year-old mother, wearing a bright yellow suit and a jaunty beret, left her wheelchair and hobbled across the courtroom.

After she was helped into the witness box, Simpson smiled adoringly as she gave jurors a brief biography of her hard life as a divorced mother of four, recounted Simpson's recovery from rickets as a child and told them how she, her son and other family members clung together the night after the killings.

"We were gripping each other," she said.

She also remembered one person who sat apart from the others: Ronald Shipp, who later testified for the prosecution that Simpson confided that night he had had dreams of killing his ex-wife and asked how long it would take for police to do DNA analysis of his blood.

Simpson in 1973 with his first wife, Marguerite, and their children Jason and Arnelle.

AP Photo

Defense Opens

It was family day at the O.J. Simpson trial. The defense chose to open its case with an outpouring of love from the Simpson women—daughter Arnelle, sisters Shirley Baker and Carmelita Simpson-Durio and mother Eunice. They dressed in the same color—shades of yellow and gold—in a show of solidarity.

With their warm recollections, the courtroom seemed transformed, as if everyone was sitting around the fireplace trading family memories. Mrs. Simpson remembered her son as a sickly baby troubled by rickets. Shirley, always the big sister, told of comforting her brother after the murders, holding his hand and applying cold compresses to his head. Carmelita recalled the days of siege when news crews surrounded the Simpson home.

But it was Arnelle who made her father smile when she told jurors proudly: "I was born the same day my dad won the Heisman Trophy."

Defense attorney Robert Shapiro surrounded by the media as he arrives at the Criminal Courts Building in downtown Los Angeles.

Photo Kevork Djansezian

"He appeared to be spaced," Mrs. Simpson said of Shipp, who was at the bar in the family room drinking beer.

Mrs. Simpson took the stand after her daughter and granddaughter told jurors that Shipp was drinking that night and offered sympathetic portraits of Simpson's demeanor on June 13, 1994. All three women were wearing shades of gold.

Mrs. Simpson told jurors that she suffers from rheumatoid arthritis. She said Simpson has the worst case among family members, bolstering the defense contention that Simpson was too crippled to kill two people.

Earlier, Arnelle Simpson said although her father's estate was equipped with a tennis court, he hadn't played in years because of arthritis in his knees and wrists.

Arnelle Simpson, 26, was led through a point-by-point rebuttal of portions of the prosecution case, countering damaging accounts by Shipp and detectives who went to Simpson's estate and woke her up early the morning the bodies were found.

Composed and soft-spoken, she used the words "shocked," "upset," "emotional," "out of control" and "distraught" as she was asked repeatedly by defense attorney Johnnie Cochran Jr. to describe her father's demeanor when he heard his ex-wife had been slain.

"He was very upset," she said of a phone conversation with him while he was in Chicago.

"He was crying. He was saying, 'Arnelle, I don't understand this.' "

"Had you at any time in your 25 years heard your father sound like that?" Cochran asked.

"No," she said.

Simpson rushed back to Los Angeles and that night, she said, friends and relatives gathered at the former football star's Brentwood mansion to comfort him. He sat on a sofa holding his mother's hand as TV newscasts reported the murders.

"He was crying off and on," Ms. Simpson said. "We were watching the news, and he kept talking to the TV, saying, 'I can't believe this.' "

She said Shipp, who has been portrayed as a hanger-on by the defense, was never alone with her father the night after the killings.

Scheck cross-examines prosecution witness William Bodziak as, from left, Hank Goldberg, Clark, Shapiro and Darden look on.

Photo Reed Saxon

Simpson with Heisman. "I was born the same day my dad won the Heisman Trophy," testified Arnelle.

AP Photo

When Simpson retired to his bedroom, his sisters, Mrs. Simpson-Durio and Shirley Baker, accompanied him upstairs. Arnelle later joined them.

"He was lying down and my Aunt Shirley was putting a cold face towel over his head," Arnelle Simpson said.

"How did he seem to you?" Cochran asked.

"Very tired, lifeless," she said.

Mrs. Simpson-Durio, who followed her niece to the stand, testified that she thought Shipp was "high" that night, but did say that Shipp went up to Simpson's bedroom for about two minutes.

With the start of the defense case, the tone of the trial changed from grim details of death to a happier family album of the Simpson household.

Arnelle Simpson recalled trips to New York to visit with her father during his sportscaster days, her own graduation from Howard University and her return to the family mansion where her father built living quarters for her and her brother Jason. And she told how Nicole Brown Simpson came running when she heard that a family dog had been found dead in the swimming pool. Together, she said, they buried the animal in the front yard.

Ms. Simpson also reminded jurors of her father's glories when Cochran elicited her birth date.

"I was born the same day my dad won the Heisman Trophy," she said, smiling.

Ms. Simpson's appearance clearly marked a high point for her father, who exchanged smiles with her several times.

Jurors watched Ms. Simpson closely and began scribbling copious notes almost from the moment she took the stand.

Her testimony was seen as crucial in reconstructing the hours after detectives entered Simp-

Cochran and Shapiro had a stormy relationship.

Photo Chris Pizzello

son's estate and notified her of the slayings, setting in motion events that would ultimately lead to his arrest.

In carefully crafted questioning, Cochran led her through the moves made by the detectives who came to the house, by houseguest Brian "Kato" Kaelin and her own actions in the crucial hours that followed.

Although she wasn't allowed to relate Simpson's remarks because they are considered hearsay, she conveyed his distress and the fact that he called back to ask about his two small children.

Ms. Simpson left the stand after a gentle cross-examination by prosecutor Marcia Clark, who sought to cast doubt on her recollection of phone calls from her father.

September 5, 1995

Los Angeles (AP)

Fuhrman was accused by the defense of being a racist cop capable of planting evidence against Simpson.

Photo Reed Saxon

Detective Mark Fuhrman

By the time the trial was over, the name Mark Fuhrman had become almost as famous as O.J. Simpson—but in an entirely different context. The transformation of Fuhrman from clean-cut, handsome, straight-talking witness to racist, expletive-spewing bigot was the trial's biggest shocker.

On the day that Fuhrman's hate-filled tapes were played in court for the first time, the jury was absent but the world was listening in. It was as if all of us in the courtroom were under bombardment by this outpouring of racist venom.

It brought back memories of another trial and another landmark piece of electronic evidence—the videotapes of black motorist Rodney King being pummeled by a group of white officers. It occurred to me then that the Fuhrman tapes were the audio equivalent of the Rodney King videotape and would have the same powerful impact.

Los Angeles Police Detective Mark Fuhrman shows the jury a plastic bag found in Simpson's white Bronco.

Photo Nick Ut

O J. SIMPSON'S JURORS heard for the first time Tuesday Detective Mark Fuhrman uttering in his own words a racist slur, and heard testimony that the star prosecution witness advocated killing blacks.

Members of the jury, which includes nine blacks, appeared shaken as the word Fuhrman denied using during the past 10 years resounded on a scratchy tape.

In a stunning climax to a battle over the tapes, Simpson's lawyers persuaded the judge to change an earlier ruling and allow the jury to hear a passage in which Fuhrman spoke of women police officers:

"They don't do anything. They don't go out there and initiate a contact with some 6-foot-5 nigger that's been in prison for seven years pumping weights," the voice on the tape said.

"Was that his voice?" defense attorney Johnnie Cochran Jr. asked screenwriter Laura Hart McKinny.

"Yes," she said.

Jurors also were read a transcript of Fuhrman saying, "We have no niggers where I grew up."

McKinny suggested to jurors that Fuhrman's 40 other times he used the word were even worse.

"When Officer Fuhrman used the word 'nigger,' it was in a very casual, ordinary pattern of speech," she told jurors. "It was nothing extraordinary. It was part of conversation."

McKinny was the third witness of the day to tell them about Fuhrman's use of the epithet.

The others described their encounters with Fuhrman in the 1980s, telling jurors how he used the word and advocated killing all blacks.

When testifying in March about finding a bloody glove on Simpson's property, Fuhrman told jurors he hadn't used that word in the past decade.

As the majority-black jury listened attentively,

witness Natalie Singer quoted Fuhrman as telling her: " 'The only good nigger is a dead nigger.' "

Earlier, Kathleen Bell told how the former detective said he'd like to kill all blacks, and that interracial romance disgusted him.

" 'If I had my way I'd gather—all the niggers would be gathered together and burned,' " Bell, choking back tears, quoted Fuhrman as saying.

Jurors appeared sickened and troubled during McKinny's testimony. Some bit their lips. A middle-aged black man recoiled when McKinny said Fuhrman used the word 42 times; others stared intently at a screen as the scratchy excerpt was played and a transcript was displayed.

Some raised their eyebrows and gave knowing, troubled looks when McKinny testified that she did not say anything in protest when Fuhrman continued to use the epithet.

Prosecutor Marcia Clark sat with a glum expression, her hands folded across her chest.

Tuesday's testimony, the first jurors heard in eight days, followed last week's ruling that disallowed most of Fuhrman's tape-recorded use of the epithet and his descriptions of police brutality.

Admission of the testimony was a triumph for defense lawyer F. Lee Bailey, who has sought to expose Fuhrman as a racist so consumed with hatred he would frame a black former football star for the June 12, 1994, murders of his white ex-wife and her friend.

It was a shattering defeat for prosecutors, who barely cross-examined Bell and Singer about Fuhrman's comments.

Before McKinny was called, prosecutor Christopher Darden fought to limit the number of witnesses who would testify about Fuhrman's racial comments.

"These are horrible, horrible things that were said," Darden argued outside the jury's presence. "It takes us to a higher level of emotionalism."

Bailey shot back: "Suddenly they have a queasy stomach because they are not in a position to call the witnesses liars."

Darden, who is black, said he knew the hateful power of the epithet but said it should not distract from the charges against Simpson in the murders of Nicole Brown Simpson and Ronald Goldman.

Robert Shapiro was the attorney the public first associated with the Simpson trial.

Photo Nick Ut

"This is not the trial of the people versus Fuhrman, not yet," Darden said.

The defense, however, was unrelenting in its attempt to undermine Fuhrman's credibility. Cochran persuaded Judge Lance Ito to allow a black man to testify that Fuhrman harassed him, arrested him and called him the same epithet.

The man was due on the stand Wednesday and the defense has promised to bring back Fuhrman and confront him under oath before they rest their case.

In his unexpected decision to substitute one of Fuhrman's comments, Ito acknowledged that after he selected the "most sanitized usage" of the epithet, he didn't ensure it was audible.

Outside jurors' presence, defense attorney Gerald Uelmen argued that Fuhrman has committed perjury on at least five instances and asked for the chance to confront Fuhrman with his taped statements as well as police photographs the defense contends were covered up to protect Fuhrman.

"I don't think we have plumbed the depths of the hatefulness and spite of Mark Fuhrman," Uelmen said.

Clark angrily responded that the defense was being allowed to "spread enough venom in this courtroom to sink a battleship."

She admitted that jurors now "will view Mr. Fuhrman as a racist," but said she was worried that they would be so inflamed they would not be able to even consider whether Fuhrman could have planted a bloody glove on Simpson's estate, as the defense has alleged.

"It's enough, your honor," Clark implored the judge. "It's enough."

Later, police photographer Rolf Rokahr told the jury he took pictures of Fuhrman pointing at evidence in the pre-dawn darkness of June 13, 1994, before Fuhrman went to Simpson's estate, not after he returned. The defense says this conflicts with Fuhrman's account and suggests he took evidence to Simpson's estate to "create probable cause."

Singer, who met Fuhrman in 1987 because her roommate was dating his police partner, was asked if she was more offended by Fuhrman's words or manner.

"When he says the things he says, it's . . . bolstered and held up and pushed out of his mouth with hatred and arrogance and despicability," she said. "And that's what hurts . . . combined with the words."

Singer and Bell said they recognized Fuhrman on TV after he testified at Simpson's preliminary hearing more than a year ago, and they began making phone calls.

Bell said she tried to reach both sides but made contact with the defense first.

"I didn't want someone to be tried without all the information, and I thought that there might be some reason that they need to know that Mark Fuhrman said these things to me," Bell testified.

The sequestered jurors took notes during the testimony, a contrast to their recent non-response to other witnesses.

September 7, 1995

Los Angeles (AP)

O J. SIMPSON'S DEFENSE went to the brink of resting Thursday and decided not to call Simpson, saying his testimony would prolong the trial and wasn't necessary to answer a prosecution case "in shambles."

The defense strategy to end with a reminder that Detective Mark Fuhrman had lied to the jury was scuttled at the last minute by a prosecution maneuver that could throw a key decision into an appeals court.

Attorney F. Lee Bailey told *The Associated Press* that Simpson's lawyers advised him not to take the witness stand in light of Fuhrman's tape-recorded statements about racism and police wrongdoing.

"With the case in shambles, this just wasn't necessary," Bailey said. "I didn't see what was left to be gained, when you have the chief witness, a law enforcement officer, refusing to testify because he might incriminate himself."

Defense attorney Robert Shapiro said later: "O.J. has always wanted to testify in this case. He realizes like all of us that this jury is weary and his testimony would prolong the case two to three weeks, and he's more anxious than any of us to get a verdict in this case."

Bailey said the decision wasn't made until recent disclosures thrust Fuhrman and tapes of his racist comments back into the forefront, climaxing in Fuhrman's dramatic appearance Wednesday.

Outside the jury's presence, Fuhrman invoked his Fifth Amendment protections against self-incrimination when the defense asked him whether he planted evidence against Simpson.

On Thursday, the defense sought to recall Fuhrman as its final witness and force him to again invoke his Fifth Amendment right to remain silent, but this time in front of the jury.

Judge Lance Ito refused but said he would tell jurors that Fuhrman was "unavailable" to testify. Prosecutors strenuously objected that they were being denied a fair trial, and the judge gave them time to file an emergency appeal.

Prosecutor Marcia Clark said she feared the jury would speculate about Fuhrman's absence even though they wouldn't be told he invoked the Fifth Amendment.

After weary jurors spent yet another day on hold while attorneys argued about Fuhrman, the judge told the panelists: "The good news is that the end is in sight. The bad news is I've got a lot of work that I have to do out of your presence."

The jurors, who have been sequestered since January 11, were told the defense would rest its case Monday and the prosecution's rebuttal would begin immediately. The judge indicated deliberations could begin in about two weeks.

Jurors never looked worse than they did when the judge broke the bad news. Jurors had dazed expressions. Some clenched their jaws. Some frowned or were grim-faced; one woman in the front row smiled broadly.

Fuhrman's lawyer, meanwhile, publicly apologized for the former detective's racist comments, made during interviews with an aspiring screenwriter from 1985 to 1994.

"All I can tell you is that Mark Fuhrman regrets the inconvenience and harm that he has caused a lot of innocent people to suffer," attorney Darryl Mounger told KCBS TV. "That's all I can really tell you. . . . He's sorry, and I don't know if that's enough."

And across the country, the U.S. Justice Department opened an inquiry into whether Fuhrman and fellow officers manufactured evidence

Fuhrman's path at Simpson's home

Los Angeles Police Detective Mark Fuhrman, once a key to the prosecution's case against O.J. Simpson, is now at the heart of the defense contention that Simpson was framed. Fuhrman testified months ago that he found a bloody glove at Simpson's estate. The defense argues Fuhrman planted the glove in a few moments he spent alone.

The morning after the murders:

- - - - Fuhrman alone
——— Fuhrman accompanied

2 Fuhrman walks alone to Bronco, notices it is parked haphazardly and finds what looks like bloodstains on door. He alerts other detectives, who come and investigate.

1 Fuhrman and detectives Philip Vannatter, Tom Lange and Mark Phillips arrive at Simpson's mansion shortly after 5 a.m. No one answers the intercom buzzer.

3 Vannatter decides to enter residence at about 5:50 a.m. Fuhrman goes over wall and opens gate.

6 Detectives knock on door of houseguest Brian Kaelin's room. He tells detectives he heard a thumping noise the previous night.

7 Fuhrman stays with Kaelin in his room. Detectives Vannatter, Lange and Phillips visit daughter Arnelle Simpson's room.

5 The four detectives walk around back of house.

8 Fuhrman and Kaelin enter house together. Kaelin is told to wait at bar.

4 Detectives ring bell at front door and get no answer.

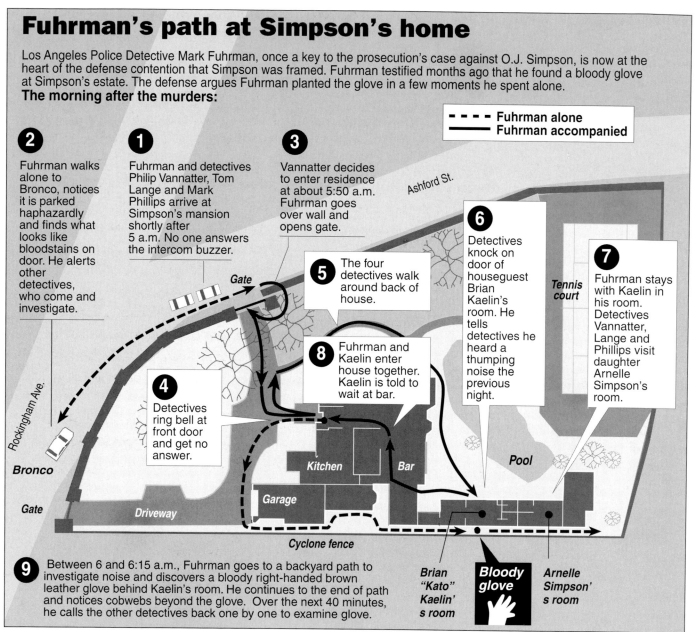

Ashford St. / Tennis court / Gate / Rockingham Ave. / Bronco / Gate / Driveway / Garage / Kitchen / Bar / Pool / Cyclone fence / Brian "Kato" Kaelin's room / Bloody glove / Arnelle Simpson's room

9 Between 6 and 6:15 a.m., Fuhrman goes to a backyard path to investigate noise and discovers a bloody right-handed brown leather glove behind Kaelin's room. He continues to the end of path and notices cobwebs beyond the glove. Over the next 40 minutes, he calls the other detectives back one by one to examine glove.

AP/Karl Gude, Karl Tate

and targeted blacks for arrest, as his taped conversations suggested.

Clark, denied the opportunity to cross-examine Simpson, at one point said that if Ito allowed Fuhrman to retake the stand, the judge should instruct jurors that Simpson as well invoked his Fifth Amendment right against self-incrimination by evading the witness stand.

"That's outrageous," Bailey fumed outside court. "Marcia Clark wants to throw out the Constitution because she's in a bad mood."

Jurors were told at the start of the case that Simpson was under no obligation to testify and didn't even have to present any defense. The burden of proof in criminal cases is on the prosecution.

Clark also argued that the defense had played unfairly when they asked Fuhrman if he had planted evidence, knowing he would be forced to stay silent once he had refused to answer previous questions.

"I don't stand in defense of Mark Fuhrman. But you've got somebody on the ropes," she said. "He's taken every hit he can. And they get up and ask him a question they know he can't answer."

Defense attorney Gerald Uelmen said the jury has a right to all information that would help them assess Fuhrman's credibility, and Fuhrman's refusal to testify was critical. Fuhrman's witness stand appearance came during a hearing on a defense motion to suppress a bloody glove and other evidence collected by Fuhrman and other detectives the day after the bodies of Nicole Brown Simpson and Ronald Goldman were found.

Ito rejected the defense bid first thing Thursday, saying Fuhrman's explanation for entering Simpson's estate without a warrant can still be trusted because it was confirmed by other detectives.

"The testimony of Fuhrman . . . is corroborated by the testimony of other witnesses," Ito wrote in a two-page ruling.

September 19, 1995

Los Angeles (AP)

TWO MOB INFORMANTS turned up at the O.J. Simpson trial Tuesday, telling how the lead detective told them Simpson was the first suspect in the double murders because "the husband is always the suspect."

The testimony by Larry Fiato and his brother Craig left jurors wide-eyed and stood in contrast to that of Detective Philip Vannatter, who was called back as a witness earlier in the day.

Los Angeles Police Detectives Tom Lange, left, and Philip Vannatter during a news conference.

Photo Eric Draper

The defense targeted Vannatter as part of an overall attack on law enforcement, trying to show that he was one of many investigators who in a "rush to judgment" assumed Simpson was the killer and later lied to cover their motives for a warrantless search of his estate.

Vannatter insisted he didn't consider Simpson a suspect when he and other detectives entered Simpson's estate hours after the bodies of Nicole Brown Simpson and Ronald Goldman were discovered.

Vannatter did concede that he spoke with the Fiatos, adding: "If something was taken out of context, if something was said in jest, I can't answer to that."

The brothers, testifying in a courtroom blocked out to TV and audio coverage to protect their safety, made it clear they were reluctant witnesses and said they had only vague memories of their conversations with Vannatter. Under questioning, however, their memories were quickly refreshed. News media lawyers fought the blackout on broadcast coverage but lost, and TV audiences missed two of the trial's most memorable witnesses. The Fiato brothers, reputed Mafia figures who began testifying for the government about 12 years ago, might have come straight from central casting.

Larry, a burly, mustachioed man with gray hair, settled into the witness chair as if he had been there many times. Craig—nicknamed "Tony the Animal"—had snow-white hair, a black goatee, a gold hoop earring and a gruff voice.

As spectators waited in hushed anticipation, the doors swung open and in walked Larry Fiato wearing a black-and-white checked vest over a black sweater. He was about to take the stand when Judge Lance Ito realized he had forgotten to summon the jurors.

After the jury assembled, Fiato testified he had been a government-co-operating witness for 11 years—although neither he nor his brother ever specifically mentioned any mob connection to the jury.

Under questioning by defense attorney Robert Shapiro, he recalled a meeting with Vannatter, Vannatter's partner, a deputy district attorney and Fiato's brother Craig at a hotel room in January.

Shapiro asked what Vannatter told him.

"It was something to the effect that he went over there as Mr. Simpson was a suspect," Larry Fiato said.

A month later, Fiato said, he was sharing a smoke with Vannatter at the courthouse when the detective jokingly made a similar statement.

Later, Fiato said, "There's no doubt in my mind he said that," and he suggested that Vannatter often talked to relieve stress and "get this stuff off (his) chest."

Craig Fiato, an imposing figure in gray silk slacks, a black jacket and brightly printed tie, at first denied he heard Vannatter say anything. He answered attorney Johnnie Cochran Jr.'s questions with a terse, "Nope," so many times that Cochran finally asked, "Are you Craig Fiato?" "I sure am," he said.

Confronted with his own transcribed statements to the district attorney's office, Fiato's memory was refreshed and he told jurors, "I heard Detective Vannatter saying, 'The husband is always the suspect.' He didn't say O.J. Simpson."

Jurors' eyes were fixated on the witnesses as they spoke. Some panelists took notes and chuckled with the audience at light moments during the testimony.

September 19, 1995

In every gruesome melodrama, comic relief is welcome. And so it was when Craig "Tony the Animal" Fiato and his bulky brother, Larry, took the stand. Craig with his gold earring and lizard boots, and Larry in his checkered vest, were playing their mobster roles to the hilt.

In a touch of irony, this most movie-like scene in the long trial was the one TV viewers didn't see. Judge Ito, yielding to the brothers' claim they would be in danger if televised, pulled the plug on TV coverage while they testified. One can only imagine Ito's reaction that evening when the Fiato brothers turned up in a pre-recorded network TV interview, their faces exposed for all the world to see.

Los Angeles Superior Court Judge Lance Ito yells in court during the Simpson trial.

Photo Eric Draper

September 21, 1995

Los Angeles (AP)

A BOLD DEFENSE PLAN to ask O.J. Simpson's jurors for an all-or-nothing verdict was snuffed out Thursday when the judge ruled the panel may consider a lesser charge of second-degree murder.

Arguing that the instruction will "undercut the defense," attorney Gerald Uelmen insisted the only options should be guilty of first-degree murder or innocent in the slashing deaths of Nicole Brown Simpson and Ronald Goldman.

"It invites the jury to compromise," Uelmen said. "We are objecting in the strongest possible terms."

But in a hearing to tie up final matters outside the jury's presence, Judge Lance Ito accepted prosecution arguments that Goldman was an unintended victim who was in the wrong place at the wrong time and Ms. Simpson may have been slain in a moment of rage and passion.

Such circumstances would weigh against the premeditation and deliberation needed for a first-degree murder conviction.

"I don't think there's any reasonable interpretation that would not indicate that Mr. Goldman's presence at the crime scene was by sheer chance," Ito said.

Prosecutors said outside court they would seek first-degree verdicts on both victims, but they argued that the evidence clearly supports the lesser option in Goldman's killing.

"A jury may find that the evidence is not sufficient beyond a reasonable doubt to convince them the defendant weighed the pros and cons of his actions," prosecutor Brian Kelberg said. But, he argued, Simpson could have killed "in a moment of sheer anger and rage."

"They have to look at what role rage and anger played."

Second-degree murder carries a maximum sentence of 15 years to life in prison with possible parole. First-degree murder carries a sentence of 25 years to life. If Simpson is convicted of multiple murder—a special circumstance—he faces life without parole.

Analysts saw the instruction as a stinging defeat for Simpson.

"It hurts because one of the concerns would be a compromise verdict in this case by jurors who may feel sympathy for Simpson but want to convict him of something," Loyola University law professor Laurie Levenson said. "This gives them something."

With testimony completed and both sides poised to rest their cases when jurors return to court Friday, the defense endured a series of other setbacks.

Ito rejected almost all of the 38 special instructions suggested by the defense.

He did approve his own special instruction about his decision to allow a prosecution witness to testify about a dream. Simpson acquaintance Ronald Shipp told jurors that after the murders, Simpson confided that he had had dreams of killing his ex-wife.

Ito acknowledged that allowing the testimony could be "a significant problem" if there is a conviction.

He said jurors would be told they must disregard the dream statement if they find either that it wasn't made or that it was expressing "unconscious thoughts."

The judge drew laughter when he asked Kelberg jokingly if he was objecting to the instruction because "Shipp happens."

In another defense setback, the California Supreme Court denied an appeal that jurors be told more about why retired detective Mark

Fuhrman wasn't called back to testify after they heard a tape of him uttering a racial slur in contradiction to his trial testimony.

Fuhrman invoked the Fifth Amendment protection against self-incrimination outside the jury's presence when asked whether he planted evidence. The defense wanted jurors to be told he was "unavailable" to return and that they could consider that in weighing his truthfulness.

Ito also refused to allow an instruction that would have highlighted Fuhrman's explosive role and given jurors permission to throw out all of his testimony if they found he testified falsely about anything.

Instead, Ito will tell them they may distrust the testimony of a witness who is "willfully false in one material part of his or her testimony" and they may even reject the entire testimony "unless, from all the evidence, you believe the probability of truth favors his or her testimony in other particulars."

Ito also rejected proposed defense instructions that would have told jurors to determine whether blood, fiber and hair evidence was contaminated before they can consider its relevance.

He disallowed a defense instruction that testimony about the statistical probability of DNA "matches" with a defendant's blood type doesn't determine the likelihood of whether the defendant committed a crime.

That ruling was visibly upsetting to defense DNA attorney Barry Scheck, who threw down his legal pad, crumpled a piece of paper and threw it across the room at the lunch break. He left the court muttering, "I don't know how many ways you can get (expletive)."

A key defense theory is that a cornerstone of the prosecution case—blood evidence—was contaminated and test results shouldn't be trusted. The defense also has pressed a theory that blood was planted to frame Simpson.

The argument on second-degree murder was pivotal to the defense, which argued that premeditation was a necessary element of the crimes.

"The position of the defendant is that, yes, these are premeditated murders—that the defendant did not commit," Uelmen said.

Kelberg said the theory that Goldman was killed merely because he was "in the wrong place at the wrong time" suggests second-degree murder. Uelmen disagreed.

"There is no evidence that suggests which of these victims, or both of them, were the target of the perpetrator," Uelmen said. "It's just as plausible . . . to suggest that Nicole Brown Simpson was in the wrong place at the wrong time when somebody came to murder Ron Goldman." But Ito said the evidence showed that Goldman had other plans for that night—going to a nightclub with a friend—and only went to Ms. Simpson's condominium to return glasses that her mother had left at the restaurant where Goldman worked.

Mezzaluna, the restaurant where Goldman worked as a waiter and where Nicole Brown Simpson ate her last meal.

Photo Michael Caulfield

September 22, 1995

Los Angeles (AP)

WITH HIS TRIAL NEARING ITS CLIMAX, O.J. Simpson rose in court Friday and seized the chance to tell the world, but not his jury: "I did not, could not and would not have committed this crime."

Johnnie Cochran.

AP Photo

Simpson addresses the court before both the prosecution and defense rested.

Photo Reed Saxon

Then, 361 days after jury selection began, lawyers rested their cases and jurors in one of the most sensational murder trials in U.S. history were read the law.

Exhibiting the confidence and aplomb he learned as a TV sportscaster, Simpson delivered a speech that seemed targeted to the court of public opinion.

Judge Lance Ito had asked Simpson to state for the record his decision not to testify in his own defense. Simpson's lawyers, ever mindful of the TV audience, maneuvered their client into a position to speak out.

Should the jury be unable to reach a decision, odds are that members of the next jury panel saw the statement.

"Good morning, your honor," Simpson said. "As much as I would like to address some of the misrepresentations about myself, and my Nicole, and our life together, I am mindful of the mood and the stamina of this jury.

"I have confidence, a lot more it seems than Miss Clark has, of their integrity and that they will find as the record stands now, that I did not, could not and would not have committed this crime."

Prosecutor Marcia Clark, suggesting a defense plan to manipulate public opinion and perhaps send a message to jurors through their families, had implored the judge not to let Simpson speak.

"This is an attempt to get testimony before the jury without cross-examination," Clark said. "Please don't do this, your honor. I beg you."

Ito assented to defense attorney Johnnie Cochran Jr.'s plea that "he has a right to speak to the waiver. They can't stop him."

But as Simpson began to talk about his children and how much he misses them, the judge cut him off.

"I have four kids. Two kids I haven't seen in a year. They ask me every week, 'Dad, how much longer?,' I want this trial over," Simpson said.

In the front row, Simpson's grown daughter, Arnelle, sobbed.

Across the room, victim Ronald Goldman's father clenched his hands into fists and muttered, "Murderer. Murderer."

"Mr. Simpson," the judge said, interrupting the monologue, "You do understand your right to testify as a witness and you choose to rest your case at this time?"

Simpson nodded.

"All right. Thank you very much, sir," Ito said. A furious Clark demanded that Simpson immediately take the stand and let her question him, but the judge didn't respond.

Cochran made a routine motion to acquit the 48-year-old Simpson of charges that he murdered Nicole Brown Simpson and her friend on June 12, 1994. The motion was quickly denied.

The jury then was summoned, and, at last, both sides announced they were resting their cases.

"I'm very pleased to say that we have no further testimony to present at this time, and as difficult as it is, the defense does rest at this time," Cochran declared.

Clark told the jury: "We ask the court to receive all of the people's exhibits, and the people rest."

Ito spent the next 45 minutes instructing jurors in the law and told them they will return Tuesday to hear final arguments on the anniversary of the day jury selection began.

The 10 women and two men on the jury, along with two alternates, have been sequestered

The defendant with Shapiro.

AP Photo

at a hotel since January 11. The judge has cited their growing impatience as a reason to end the trial quickly.

The jurors smiled broadly and nodded their heads vigorously when Ito asked if they would be willing to work nights next week to conclude the arguments and begin deliberations. "Yes! Yes!" one of them said.

"We have one unanimous decision already," Ito quipped.

In clear, concise terms, he explained to them that if they acquitted Simpson of first-degree murder, they still could convict him of second-degree murder.

He spoke of such legal terms as premeditation, express malice and reasonable doubt.

"You are the sole judges of the believability of a witness," he said, explaining they may consider a witness's demeanor, bias, motive and character in assessing truthfulness. But he never mentioned the name of Detective Mark Fuhrman, having turned down a defense bid to mention his unavailability for further testimony.

Ito told jurors about considering DNA evidence, evaluating expert testimony and weighing the impact of laboratory errors on the validity of scientific evidence.

Simpson sat at the counsel table still as a statue, his brow furrowed, staring at the judge during the reading. Once, when the elements of murder were being discussed, he appeared to flinch.

The Brown family was not in court for Simpson's statement.

Ms. Simpson's father, Lou Brown, told CNBC's "Rivera Live" that Simpson's comment about his children was only partially true.

"I asked him five or six months ago if he wanted the kids brought to the jail for a visit. He said definitely not," Brown said. "He was very emphatic. He didn't want them to see him in jail because then he'd have to start explaining why he was there."

Goldman's father was seething when he left the courtroom.

"If he had a statement to make he should have gotten on the damn stand and said something and not been a coward and been unable to have the prosecution question him," Goldman said, his voiced quavering. Then, referring to Simpson's statement about missing his children, Goldman said: "I will never see my son again."

It was Simpson's longest public statement since before his arrest on June 17, 1994, after he led a phalanx of police cars on a 60-mile-long, slow-speed chase.

During the trial, prosecutors called 72 primary and rebuttal witnesses, while the defense called 53 main case witnesses and one rebuttal witness. So the jury of nine blacks, two whites and one Hispanic heard from 126 witnesses since testimony started on January 31.

O.J. Simpson—Profile

The Faces of O.J.
Tough Kid, Football Hero, Media Star, Murder Suspect

Simpson carries the Olympic torch through the streets of Santa Monica after the flame's arrival for the 1984 Summer Olympics.
AP Photo

These are the pictures of an American icon.

At 6, he smiles shyly into the camera, a little boy in a too-big suit, sleeves brushing his knuckles, pants billowing around his ankles.

Just over a decade later, the tentative smile has widened into the confident grin of a football star on the rise.

At thirtysomething, the by-now-famous face flashes the megawatt beam of a pitchman as he lopes through airports and mugs through films of varying quality.

On June 17, 1994, the smile vanishes, replaced by the empty, stunned stare of a man accused of murdering his ex-wife and her friend.

Tough kid turned football hero turned media star, O.J. Simpson has worn many faces. On September 26, 1994, he assumed yet another identity: a man on trial for his freedom.

Don't feel sorry for me. I've had a great life, great friends. Please think of the real O.J. and not this lost person.

— *Letter left behind when Simpson fled police,*
June 17, 1994

In the beginning, there was the charm.

Joe Bell, who played football with Simpson at Galileo High School in San Francisco, remembers watching Simpson hone his people-winning skills at the gates of the '49ers football stadium, wheedling extra tickets from softhearted fans and then promptly scalping them.

"You had to convince some guy that was coming to the game who had an extra ticket that you were a poor kid that wanted to see the game, so at a very young age we learned to court public sympathy," Bell says.

From the inside, he says, Simpson's well-documented rise over rickets, an absentee father and the Potrero Hill housing projects was gradual, not the march to destiny it appears in retrospect.

Reality hit one day toward the end of Simpson's days at the University of Southern California when, for grins, the two added up the money Simpson could make if he accepted all the speaking engagements that were pouring in.

"I said, 'Man, you are on your way,'" Bell recalled.

Simpson's football exploits are legend: Heisman Trophy, 1968; Buffalo Bills top pick, 1969; National Football League record of 2,003 yards rushing, 1973; Pro Football Hall of Fame, 1985.

Off the field, there were more triumphs: his briefcase-toting commercials for Hertz, his career as a football commentator, and roles in a string of movies that were less than Oscar-caliber but served to cement his nice-guy image.

It all added up to a lifestyle far removed from the winding streets of Potrero Hill.

At one point in my life my purpose was to be known. To be liked and known by people.

— *Interview with the* San Francisco Examiner, *March 1978*

Some said Simpson had moved too far from his roots. There were criticisms that he surrounded himself with white friends, took diction lessons to Anglicize his speech and was a scarce figure in the old neighborhood.

Simpson said those who faulted him didn't really know him.

In 1974, when a San Francisco newspaper said his movie *The Klansman,* would set "race relations back 50 years," he responded, "What do they mean by race relations? I don't trip off the fact that I'm black and you're white. I don't go into the Buffalo Bills and say, 'Let's establish race relations.' That's 10 years old."

But if there were fissures in the genial image, they were largely obscured by the patina of success.

There was the $5 million estate in the exclusive Brentwood area of Los Angeles, the Rolls-Royce, winters in Aspen and summers at an oceanfront house in Orange County.

The boy who once scooped up abandoned stadium seat cushions for the pennies-back deposit now, according to his houseguest Brian "Kato" Kaelin, sometimes carried nothing smaller than a $100 bill.

Everyone sees this golden hero, or golden nice guy, but I have my faults, too.

Interview with the San Francisco Examiner, *March 1978.*

Simpson's 11-year marriage to high school sweetheart Marguerite Whitley broke up in 1979, the same year their daughter, 23-month-old Aaren, died in a swimming pool accident.

By the time of the divorce, Simpson already was deep into a relationship with Nicole Brown, an 18-year-old waitress he met at a

Beverly Hills nightclub called the Daisy. Their seven-year marriage ended in 1992, although they continued to live near each other and often were seen together at events.

The only public documentation of Simpson's temper was New Year's Day 1989, when he beat his wife and she told police, "He's going to kill me."

Simpson pleaded no contest to a charge of wife-beating, agreeing to a fine, community service and counseling. He later dismissed the altercation as "no big deal"; he pleaded no contest only to avoid more publicity.

"It was embarrassing, but because our relationship was strong and all our friends knew it and they knew what they were reading wasn't necessarily the truth, hey, we just tried to put it behind us and ignore it as much as we could," he told ESPN that year.

But as the world learned this summer, that wasn't the only time police were called to Ms. Simpson's aid.

A tape of a 911 call on October 25, 1993, reveals an enraged Simpson harassing his sobbing ex-wife as their children slept upstairs, a chilling scene from a failed marriage.

I'm not violent . . . even on the football field I try to avoid contact. I try not to hit anybody or let them hit me.

— *Interview in the* San Francisco Chronicle Datebook, *April 1974.*

Simpson with, from left, Frank Gatski, Joe Namath, Pete Rozelle and Roger Staubach when all five were inducted into the Pro Football Hall of Fame in 1985.

AP Photo

As Ms. Simpson's pleas for help were broadcast on television again and again, stark images of Simpson, the murder defendant, began to emerge at his first court appearances in June—tieless, beltless, under suicide watch, a haggard caricature of the gracious superstar.

Just as pictures captured Simpson's rise and fall—and his infamous run from justice in a white Ford Bronco, complete with cheering fans—they also documented his physical resurgence while incarcerated.

At his arraignment, he firmly declared himself "absolutely, 100 percent not guilty" and gave a thumbs-up as he left the courtroom.

Supporters said his dramatic rebound did not signify a man assuming a new persona— courageous defendant—but instead was a natural reaction.

"The media has deified O.J. as this person who was something other than human. But I knew O.J. the friend, I knew O.J. the father," Bell says. "I've seen the real, caring O.J. who would stand for hours taking pictures with people and signing autographs. I have seen the total O.J. Simpson. . . . He's incapable of doing that kind of crime."

District Attorney Gil Garcetti acknowledged from the start of this surreal case that his job would be difficult.

"There is no doubt," he said, "that O.J. Simpson, the persona, the hero, is something that most people don't want to let go."

Simpson appears with Gilda Radner, left, and Jane Curtin on "Saturday Night Live" in February 1978.

Source: NBC

September 27, 1995

KEY ARGUMENTS MADE WEDNESDAY by prosecutor Christopher Darden and defense attorney Johnnie Cochran Jr. during closing arguments in the O.J. Simpson murder trial:

Prosecution Points

FATEFUL PHONE CALL: A call to Nicole Brown Simpson the day of the murders may have pushed Simpson over the edge, Darden said. Things got even worse when Simpson's girlfriend Paula Barbieri took off for Las Vegas without telling Simpson, and when the Brown family didn't invite Simpson to dinner after a dance recital during which Ms. Simpson ignored her ex-husband.

DEADLY PLAN: After working himself up into an emotional rage because he was spurned by his ex-wife and his girlfriend, Simpson drafted a plan to solve his problems by killing Ms. Simpson: "He always blamed her, and everything was her fault," Darden said.

MURDEROUS RELIEF: With each thrust of the knife into his victims, Simpson felt better, and after the murders, Simpson was so relieved that he walked—didn't run or even jog—away from the crime scene, as evidenced by the space between the bloody shoe prints, the prosecutor said.

ROCKY RELATIONSHIP: The tensions that led to the murders started building long before June 12, 1994, said Darden, who pointed to the Simpsons' turbulent relationship. He said Ms. Simpson had been worn down by Simpson, and she stayed with him because, in the words of a song, "The strong give up and move away and the weak give up and stay."

Defense Points

NO FIT, MUST ACQUIT: Playing on the prosecution's gloves-didn't-fit fiasco, Cochran said of any evidence: "If it doesn't fit, you must acquit." He insisted that so much of the prosecution's case doesn't make sense that prosecutors couldn't prove guilt beyond a reasonable doubt.

TIMELINE: Placing the time of the murders later than the prosecution did, Cochran said Simpson wouldn't have had time to get back home and crash into a wall air-conditioner at 10:40 P.M. or 10:45 P.M., as Brian "Kato" Kaelin testified.

NO DISGUISE: Ridiculing prosecutors' suggestion that Simpson wore a dark knit cap to disguise himself, Cochran put on a similar hat and asked the jury: "Who am I?" He answered his own question, "I'm Johnnie Cochran with a knit cap on. From two blocks away, O.J. Simpson is O.J. Simpson."

DEMEANOR: Showing a videotape and a photograph of Simpson taken just hours before the murders, Cochran said the beaming, laughing Simpson didn't look anything like a killer.

Scheck and Marcia Clark.

Photo Reed Saxon

NOT ENOUGH BLOOD: Cochran said that if Simpson had committed the murders, authorities should have found even more blood at his house, including on the doors, light switches and light-colored carpeting. Also, there was not blood around the glove found behind Simpson's house.

NO WOUNDS: Cochran showed pictures of Simpson's nearly unscathed body taken in the days after the slayings, arguing that a person who attacked two people in a short time would have struggled fiercely and sustained multiple wounds, many more than the few marks seen on Simpson's hands.

BIASED WITNESS: One of the prosecution's top witnesses, glove expert Richard Rubin, was "a soldier in the prosecution army," Cochran said, noting that Rubin had mentioned in a letter to prosecutors something about a victory party.

ATONED SINS: Of the evidence of domestic violence, Cochran said the incidents were in the distant past and that Simpson had not struck his ex-wife since a fight in 1989. "O.J. Simpson is not proud of that 1989 incident. You know what? He paid his debt to that," Cochran said, referring to Simpson's no-contest plea and probation sentence.

Simpson supporter Morris Griffin, right, dares an unidentified man to take his leather gloves off during a confrontation.

Photo Nick Ut

BEATRICE PUBLIC LIBRARY
BEATRICE, NEBR. 68310

September 28, 1995

Los Angeles (AP)

I N A THUNDERING SUMMATION that rocked the court, Johnnie Cochran Jr. exhorted O.J. Simpson's mostly black jury Thursday to "do the right thing" and acquit Simpson as a message against racism and police misconduct.

When Cochran's final presentation to jurors came to a close with the words "God bless you," the judge told them prosecutor Marcia Clark would conclude her rebuttal Friday, clearing the way for the year-old trial to be placed in their hands.

Jurors appeared dazed after long days of absorbing arguments this week, and they didn't react to the judge's news.

But earlier in the day they were spellbound as Cochran, in the fevered style of a revival preacher, invoked biblical texts, referred to two key detectives as "the twin devils of deception" and told them that fate had given them a chance to change history.

"Maybe there is a reason why we're here," he said. "Maybe you're the right people at the right time at the right place to say: 'No more!'"

"Stop this cover-up! Stop this cover-up!" Cochran bellowed in the second day of his summation. "You are the consciences of this community."

Far from Los Angeles, President Clinton said he was uneasy about the racial implications of the trial.

"I'm concerned about it and I hope the American people will not let this become some symbol of the larger racial issue in our country," the president told NBC-TV in Washington.

In his final words to the jury, Cochran im-

Simpson closing arguments

Thursday, September 28, 1995

Defense

▶ Defense attorney Johnnie Cochran wrapped up his closing arguments in the style of a revival preacher. His theme was racism and police misconduct, and at one point he compared Detective Mark Fuhrman to Adolf Hitler.

▶ Defense attorney Barry Scheck told jurors they could not trust any of the DNA analysis of blood because of police contamination and tampering.

▶ Judge Lance Ito recessed court three hours early Thursday after promised by attorneys to end Friday with enough time for the judge to give his final instructions and jurors to select a foreperson and get organized. Deliberations begin Monday next week.

AP

plored jurors to acquit Simpson, invoking the image of his two small children. He stood before a wall-size blowup of Simpson and his small daughter, Sydney, and spoke of a father's love.

"Someone has taken these children's mother," he said. "I hope your decision doesn't take their father."

He listed 15 points of reasonable doubt and turned to the Bible in his final moments at the lectern. He cited sections of Proverbs dealing with false witnesses who must be punished and urged jurors to carry out God's will.

"I know you will stay the course, keep your eye on the prize and do the right thing," Cochran said.

Cochran's impassioned appeal, which en-

Cochran's Closing Argument

If race had once been a subtext in the Simpson trial, it was at the forefront by the time Johnnie Cochran Jr. rose to address the jury of 10 women and two men— nine of them black.

As Cochran summoned up his most righteous indignation, the rafters seemed to rock. Few tent revivals had ever heard a preacher of such power. One expected a chorus of hallelujahs to echo forth as he thundered: "Stop this cover-up! You are the consciences of the community."

He quoted the Bible and several major poets and philosophers and implored jurors to send Simpson home to his two small children. His appeal on racial grounds was so blatant that it brought a response from the White House where President Clinton expressed concern that the case was becoming symbolic of racial issues. But for the jury, style overcame substance. They said later that race played no role in their decision. Asked about Cochran's speech, one of them said, "It was like being in church."

raged the father of one murder victim, was followed by the cooler, scientific analysis of defense attorney Barry Scheck, who told jurors: "There is a cancer at the heart of this case."

Scheck insisted they could not trust any of the DNA analysis of blood because the samples were contaminated and tampered with in the "black hole" of the Los Angeles Police Department crime lab.

"Somebody played with this evidence," he said. "There's no doubt about it."

Using an analogy posed by forensic expert Henry Lee, Scheck compared the defense discovery of flawed evidence to finding a cockroach in a bowl of spaghetti—enough of a sign that the whole bowl is infested.

"How many cockroaches do you have to find in the bowl of spaghetti?" he asked. "This is reasonable doubt."

Cochran's emotion-packed discourse—often focused on Detective Mark Fuhrman—clearly was designed to rouse feelings of racial solidarity among the nine blacks of the 12-member jury.

The jury, which includes two whites and a Hispanic, sat mesmerized through Cochran's arguments. He was interrupted only once when a woman juror asked to go to the restroom.

"A racist is someone who has power over you," he told them. "This man would lie and set you up because of the hatred he has in his heart."

He played the sound of Fuhrman's voice speaking the infamous racial epithet that he swore to them he had not spoken in 10 years. He read to jurors every word of a letter from witness Kathleen Bell, who testified she heard Fuhrman advocate burning all blacks.

Comparing Fuhrman to Adolf Hitler and stressing the images of genocide, Cochran said the former detective targeted Simpson after learning in the 1980s that the black football star was married to a white woman.

When Nicole Brown Simpson and Ronald Goldman were found slain, he said, it presented Fuhrman with the opportunity to plant a bloody glove and other evidence to frame Simpson for the murders.

During Cochran's summation, Goldman's father, Fred, sat tapping his foot in agitation. At the break, he went before TV cameras and lashed out at Cochran.

"This man is sick," he said. "This man is a horror walking around amongst us."

"We have seen a man who perhaps is the worst kind of racist himself," Goldman told reporters, "someone who shoves racism in front of everything, someone who compares a person who speaks racist comments to Hitler, a person who murdered millions of people. This man is the worst kind of human being imaginable."

Those comments spurred the normally silent Simpson family to respond on camera with their own news conference.

"We have waited all this time, and now . . . the attorneys are telling my brother's story. And it's very shocking that once Johnnie gets up and starts telling what we feel happened that this has rocked somebody's world," Simpson's sister Carmelita Simpson-Durio said.

She was joined by her sister Shirley Baker, Simpson's two grown children and his mother.

"It's wrong, even when you're hurting, for someone to get up and personally attack our lawyers and say that they're liars," Baker said.

Jurors, sequestered since January 11, were shielded from the families' comments.

Cochran's summation was dominated by the theme of racism and police misconduct. He said Detective Philip Vannatter was Fuhrman's ally in framing Simpson and was "the man who carried the blood."

He said Vannatter's unusual decision to carry Simpson's blood sample from police headquarters, where it was drawn the day after the murders, to Simpson's estate showed he was in on the conspiracy.

In concluding his argument, Cochran gave a rallying cry for jurors to join him as soldiers in the fight against racism and inequality.

"You and I, fighting for freedom and ideals and for justice for all, must continue to expose hate and genocidal racism and these tendencies," he said. "We, then, become the guardians of the Constitution."

Outside court, Vannatter's partner and co-Simpson investigator Detective Tom Lange criticized Cochran. "The preacher," he told reporters, "has turned into a snake oil salesman."

Defense attorney Johnnie Cochran, flanked by bodyguards, arrives at the Los Angeles Criminal Courts Building.

Photo Nick Ut

September 29, 1995

Los Angeles (AP)

In the jury room

Jurors have several options as they deliberate the murder case against O.J. Simpson.

The verdict

Acquittal

Jurors unanimously decide Simpson is innocent of both murder charges. Simpson would be cleared of the charges and could not be retried.

Conviction

a. Simpson is convicted of first-degree murder on both charges.

b. Simpson is convicted of one count of first-degree murder and one count of second-degree murder.

c. Simpson is convicted of two counts of second-degree murder.

The mandatory sentence is life in prison without possibility of parole.

The mandatory sentence is 15 years to life. Parole is possible.

If Simpson is convicted, Judge Lance Ito would set a sentencing hearing, probably within 30 days. All murder convictions in California are automatically appealed.

Deadlock

Jurors cannot come to a decision. The district attorney could retry Simpson on any undecided charges. Simpson would remain jailed pending retrial.

The jury

Although 10 jurors have been dismissed since the trial began, the jury that will decide Simpson's fate is demographically similar to the original 12-person panel.

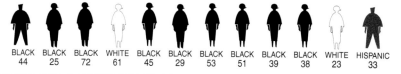

| BLACK 44 | BLACK 25 | BLACK 72 | WHITE 61 | BLACK 45 | BLACK 29 | BLACK 53 | BLACK 51 | BLACK 39 | BLACK 38 | WHITE 23 | HISPANIC 33 |

AP

A YEAR AFTER his murder trial began, the fate of O.J. Simpson was placed in the hands of 12 anonymous people Friday by a judge who ordered them to ignore lawyer warnings that "the world is watching."

The jurors were expressionless—as they have been throughout the trial—when they filed into the jury room, where they will have more than 50,000 pages of transcripts and 857 pieces of evidence to consider.

Simpson closing arguments

Friday, September 29, 1995

Prosecution

▶ With one final playing of Nicole Brown Simpson's call to a 911 operator, prosecutor Marcia Clark finished her closing argument.

▶ Judge Lance Ito told the jury to ignore the fact that "the world is watching" and arrive at a verdict dispassionately.

▶ The jurors left the courtroom and chose a foreman in mere moments. Deliberations begin Monday.

AP

The beaten face and the desperate voice of Nicole Brown Simpson were the last pieces of evidence presented as prosecutor Marcia Clark implored the majority-black panel to find the sports legend guilty of murdering his ex-wife and her friend.

As crowds gathered outside the courthouse for the climactic turn in the case that has captivated the na-tion, Judge Lance Ito told the 12 jurors inside his courtroom that their sworn duty was to "reach a just verdict regardless of the consequences."

"You are not partisans or advocates, but impartial judges of the fact," Ito said. The panel quickly chose a foreperson and then retired for the weekend without beginning formal deliberations. They were to reconvene Monday morning.

The two alternates remain under guard in case they are needed to step in.

Wesley Griswold of El Monte, California, leaves little doubt as to his choice of verdicts. This photo was taken Monday, October 2, 1995, hours before the jury reached its verdict.

Photo Bob Galbraith

Bronco Evidence

Clark points to an evidence chart during her closing argument.

Photo Reed Saxon

Three minutes after the case was submitted at 4:08 P.M. PDT on the courtroom clock, a jury room buzzer sounded three times, signaling that the foreperson had been selected.

"Maybe they've got a verdict and we can all go home," defense attorney Johnnie Cochran Jr. quipped.

Laughter erupted, breaking a palpable tension that had built during the final moment of Clark's argument as she let the victims speak for themselves through videotape and pictures.

The families of Ms. Simpson and Ronald Goldman dissolved in tears when Clark summoned up the beaten face and desperate voice of Ms. Simpson pleading for police protection from her ranting ex-husband and when an image of Goldman's bloody body flashed on the 7-foot-high courtroom screen. "Usually, I feel I'm the only one left to speak for the victims," Clark told jurors. "But Nicole and Ron are speaking to you."

She urged the 10 women and two men to hear the resignation in Ms. Simpson's voice in a 911 call and consider the words she spoke to a police detective who responded to a domestic violence call at the Simpson home six years before the murders: "He's going to kill me."

The tapes from a 1989 call and a 1993 call were played over defense objections to what lawyers called "a production" unfairly mingling unrelated evidence.

As the tapes were played, Clark displayed a montage of her case up on the screen: Ms. Simpson's beaten face in 1989, the crime scene, blood drops on Simpson's driveway, Simpson's white Bronco, a bloody glove and, finally, the slashed bodies.

She suggested that Goldman was a hero in the effort to convict his killer because, "Ron, struggling so valiantly, forced the killer to leave evidence."

"They told you with their blood, with their hair . . . that he did it—Orenthal Simpson," she said, turning to where Simpson sat impassively at the counsel table.

The judge's final instructions and the jury's departure to begin deliberations marked the end of a convulsive yearlong battle, which placed the justice system itself on trial and raised disturbing issues of racism within the Los Angeles Police Department.

The final session on Friday was as contentious as any, with Cochran and Barry Scheck peppering Clark with a fusillade of objections—

more than 60 in all—which fragmented portions of her argument.

But in the final moments, there was silence among the participants. Ms. Simpson's haunting voice filled the courtroom.

In the spectator section, her sisters Tanya and Denise Brown held their hands over their ears and wept with their mother, Juditha.

Goldman's family was in tears.

To the end, jurors were expressionless.

In the hallway before the morning session began, Mrs. Brown walked over to Simpson's frail mother, Eunice, leaned over her wheelchair and kissed her on the cheek.

Emotion also built outside the courthouse, where crowds gathered throughout the day and police put up barricades and tape. Some spectators cheered as defense attorneys arrived.

Supporters on both sides played on a theme of Cochran's closing argument: There were shirts that read, "If it doesn't fit then you must acquit," and a sign that said, "If they acquit, they're full of (expletive)."

As planned, the Sheriff's Department went on tactical alert putting deputies on call when jurors were handed the case.

Drops of blood

PROSECUTION: Lynchpin of the case; places Simpson at the crime scene; Simpson dripped blood after being wounded on left hand during murders.

Two drops of blood found at the crime scene alongside bloody footprints leading away from the slashed bodies of Nicole Brown Simpson and Ronald Goldman. DNA tests point to a match with Simpson's blood.

DEFENSE: Samples were improperly collected by sloppy investigators, then subjected to flawed testing at laboratory; DNA evidence doesn't always pass scientific and judicial muster.

Human hairs

PROSECUTION: Places Simpson at crime scene.

Hairs found in a dark knit cap and on Goldman's clothing reportedly resemble those of a black person, and crime lab tests indicate they may belong to Simpson.

DEFENSE: Means nothing more than assailant may have been a black person—roughly 10 percent of Los Angeles' population.

Bloody gloves

PROSECUTION: Links Simpson to crime scene; Simpson lost the left glove at Ms. Simpson's house during the struggle, then dropped the right glove behind the guest house while frantically trying to hide it in the dark.

One dark leather glove covered with blood was found at the crime scene; another was found behind Simpson's guest house — just below the spot where guest Kato Kaelin heard a bump in the night.

DEFENSE: Glove behind guest house could have been placed by somebody trying to frame Simpson; doesn't make sense for Simpson to have carefully ditched the weapon and his clothes and then have been so careless in disposing of a bloody glove.

Limo driver

PROSECUTION: The black person was Simpson, who had been doing something behind the house — possibly trying to hide the glove.

Limousine driver Allan Park testified Simpson didn't appear to be home when Park arrived at 10:45 p.m. June 12 to take Simpson to the airport. Park said that at about 10:56 p.m. he saw a large black person walking from the side of the house into the front door. About 15 seconds later, Park said, Simpson answered the intercom.

DEFENSE: Park's watch may have been wrong or his memory was lacking; black figure could have been anybody; even if it were Simpson, it doesn't matter since the house is, after all, his.

Kato Kaelin

PROSECUTION: Helps frame Simpson's window of opportunity; Simpson's whereabouts are unaccounted for from the time he returned from McDonald's with Kaelin at 9:40 p.m. until the limo driver first saw him.

This house guest of Simpson's was the last person to have seen Simpson before the murders.

DEFENSE: Not enough time for Simpson to drive to Ms. Simpson's house, kill two people, hide bloodied clothing and a weapon, drive home, drop a glove behind the guest house, clean up, change clothes and get into the limo.

Bloody Bronco

PROSECUTION: Shows Simpson drove the Bronco to and from the crime scene.

A small spot of blood found above driver's side door handle of Simpson's Ford Bronco. Other blood found inside the vehicle.

DEFENSE: Blood could have been left in car at any time; blood tests are flawed.

Violent past

PROSECUTION: Points to motive, showing Simpson was a man prone to jealous rages and capable of hurting Ms. Simpson.

Simpson was convicted in 1989 of beating Ms. Simpson. A former boyfriend of Ms. Simpson's testified that Simpson stalked them.

DEFENSE: Irrelevant, isolated events. The evidence's tendency to prejudice the jury outweighs any light it may shed on the case.

October 3, 1995

Los Angeles (AP)

O J. SIMPSON WAS ACQUITTED TODAY of murdering his ex-wife and her friend, a suspense-filled climax to the courtroom saga that obsessed the nation. With two words, "not guilty," the jury freed the fallen sports legend to try to rebuild a life thrown into disgrace.

Simpson looked toward the jury and mouthed, "Thank you," after the panel was dismissed.

Judge Lance Ito ordered him taken to the Sheriff's Department and released forthwith.

Simpson, who stood facing the jury, raised his right hand and motioned to the jury. He then hugged his lead defense attorney, Johnnie Cochran Jr., and his friend and attorney Robert Kardashian.

In the audience, the sister of victim Ronald Goldman broke out in sobs. Her father sat back in his seat in disbelief, then embraced his daughter.

Simpson's relatives smiled and wiped away tears. His son Jason sat in his seat, his face in his hands, shaking and sobbing. Prosecutor Marcia Clark and Christopher Darden sat stone-faced.

L.A. security

■ Police were on tactical alert, retaining morning shifts and increasing the number of day shift officers by a third.
■ Temple Street, in front of the criminal court building, was blocked off by squad cars; 20 to 30 officers were standing by.
■ Rockingham Avenue and Bundy Drive were closed off, forbidding access to O.J. Simpson's estate and Nicole Brown Simpson's condo.
■ A command center in the basement of City Hall was staffed with police and fire personnel for emergency operations.

LAPD, AP Research

Simpson with Cowlings as he arrived home after his acquittal.

Photo Reed Saxon

Shirley Baker, left, and Carmelita Simpson-Durio, Simpson's sisters, rush into the arms of defense attorney Robert Blasier at the Simpson estate.

Photo Reed Saxon

The judge thanked the jury and cautioned panelists that reporters would seek them out. Jurors said they didn't want to talk to attorneys or the media.

Simpson was cleared of the June 12, 1994, murders of his ex-wife Nicole Brown Simpson, 35, and her 25-year-old friend.

A throng outside the courthouse cheered.

The curious and an army of media began arriving early today, while police went on tactical alert to brace for possible trouble in the streets.

News helicopters roared outside. Barricades blocked the street. In the courthouse lobby, hundreds of people vied for the few precious public seats in the courtroom. As their lottery numbers were pulled, the lucky few cheered.

They came to take their place in history, to experience the verdict of the century.

It came Monday without warning. As the judge brought in the jury, two-thirds of the hottest seats in town were empty, two of the leading attorneys in the case weren't even present, and most of the media—not expecting such a swift verdict—were upstairs in the pressroom.

"Is that correct?" Ito asked the forewoman, a black woman in her early fifties who was chosen by her colleagues last week after just three minutes.

"Yes," she said.

Jaws dropped. There were gasps in the courtroom. Simpson appeared stunned, as did his attorney, Carl Douglas, a second-stringer on the legal team assigned the mundane task of sitting next to Simpson during testimony readbacks.

Arnelle Simpson and Carmelita Simpson-Durio celebrate Simpson's acquittal with balloons.

Photo Reed Saxon

Milagros Guzman, second from right, reacts as she and other pedestrians along a
New York street watch a portable TV she carries for news of the verdict.

Photo Adam Nadel

"Surprise doesn't begin to describe my feelings," Douglas said afterward.

Prosecutor Christopher Darden was there, but Clark wasn't.

Darden, asked if he could believe the rapid end to deliberations, said, "I think I have to believe it. It's happening. Nothing shocks me anymore."

Ito suggested jurors use their time before the verdict's announcement to pack and bid farewell to nearly nine months of sequestration.

"Ladies and gentlemen, have your last pleasant evening," he told them.

Jurors spent about an hour of their brief deliberations listening to a court reporter read back testimony from a limousine driver who gave Simpson a ride to the airport on the night Simpson's ex-wife and her friend were slain.

The jurors heard only testimony that prosecutors suggested they review: limousine driver Allan Park's descriptions of phone calls he made to his boss and mother and his efforts to summon a response from Simpson by ringing a bell at the gate to his Rockingham Avenue estate.

The verdict capped a legal journey as surreal—and at times as slow—as Simpson's bizarre Bronco flight from justice.

As the case moved onto one side street after another, it often seemed irrelevant that two young people were slashed to death one June night in Brentwood more than a year ago.

The case wasn't just about murder. It was about fame and wealth, love and hate, fragile egos and misdirected power. It was about the judicial system, the media, domestic violence, racism, sexism and crass opportunism.

It was Greek tragedy, afternoon soap opera and circus sideshow, all televised live and nationwide. It had heroes, villains and freaks, plot twists, suspense and anticlimaxes.

America couldn't get enough if it.

Shapiro hugs Arnelle Simpson hours after the not guilty verdict was read.

Photo Reed Saxon

Jurors—Profiles

The Jurors
and Alternates in the
O.J. Simpson Trial:

Jurors (by seat number):

1. Divorced black woman, 51, works as vendor; said she "respects (Simpson) as an individual based on his past accomplishments"; said she had a "stressful, sick feeling" when she first heard Simpson was a murder suspect; described racial discrimination against blacks as a "somewhat serious problem"; lives in South Central Los Angeles. Chosen as jury forewoman.

2. Single black woman, 25, works at a Los Angeles County hospital; said she has had no experience with domestic violence; said of both sides in the case, "Everybody has a lot to lose or gain"; alternate juror until June 6; lives in Gardena.

3. Divorced white woman, 61, retired gas company worker; said she was lone holdout in another murder case and managed to get other jurors to change their minds; alternate juror until March 17; lives in Norwalk.

4. Single Hispanic man, 33, drives Pepsi truck; said Simpson was "a great football player"; has spoken throughout sequestration about how much he misses his young son; expressed a desire to be juror in the case, saying, "If you want somebody who is honest and does believe in this court system, I'm him"; lives in East Los Angeles.

5. Married black woman, 38, works in "private hire and business"; said she had "no feelings toward Mr. Simpson" and that she never followed football; described racial discrimination against blacks as "not too serious"; lives in Bellflower.

6. Married black man, 44, marketing representative; said he thought Simpson was a good football player; described the slow-speed Bronco chase as "blown out of proportion"; said racial discrimination against blacks is a "very serious problem"; alternate juror until January 18; lives in the Mid-Wilshire section of Los Angeles.

7. Single black woman, 45, repairs computers and printers for county Superior Court; said Ms. Simpson "wasn't a saint"; said in jury selection, "If I'm not picked, I can look at it and say, they let a good one go"; alternate juror until April 5; lives in South Central Los Angeles.

8. Single black woman, 39, environmental health specialist whose father was a police officer; said the 911 tapes of Nicole Brown Simpson calling for police help as Simpson broke through her door in October 1993 "sound frightening"; one of two college graduates on jury; lives in Inglewood.

9. Divorced black woman, 53, postal clerk; described Simpson as "only human"; watched the entire slow-speed chase on television; described racial discrimination against blacks as "not too serious"; lives in South Central Los Angeles.

10. Married black woman, 29, unloads mail trucks; said she was "shocked" to hear Simpson was a murder suspect; said of the slow-speed chase, "I was scared of what the outcome might be"; said her father was "very abusive to my mother" and that she wouldn't "go for any man being abusive to me"; called racism a "somewhat serious problem"; alternate juror until June 5; lives in Compton.

11. Single white woman, 23, handles insurance claims; also said she was shocked when she heard Simpson was a suspect; called DNA "somewhat reliable" and that testing "would hold some value"; the second college graduate on panel; called racism against blacks "not too serious"; lives in Burbank.

12. Married black woman, 72, retired "cleaning officer"; said of the case, "I haven't come to no conclusion one way or the other. . . . I don't know nothing about no O.J. Simpson"; alternate juror until May 26; lives in Crenshaw District.

Alternate Jurors:

13. Married white woman, 25, former manicurist, now receptionist; married to a black man and said there is a "somewhat serious problem" of discrimination against blacks in Southern California; when asked her reaction to finding out she was in jury pool said, "It was, like, wow!"; lives in Altadena.

14. Married black man, 73, works as a security guard; described Simpson as a superb running back; "I admired his ability"; said he had experienced "many racial incidents," including one involving a white gang; indicated he didn't know much about DNA but was "willing to be taught"; lives in Inglewood.

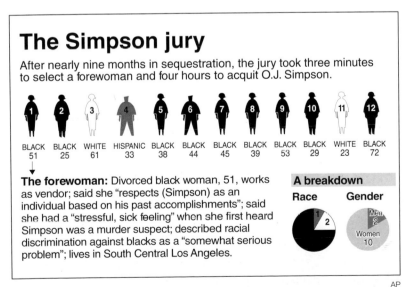

The Simpson jury

After nearly nine months in sequestration, the jury took three minutes to select a forewoman and four hours to acquit O.J. Simpson.

1	2	3	4	5	6	7	8	9	10	11	12
BLACK 51	BLACK 25	WHITE 61	HISPANIC 33	BLACK 38	BLACK 44	BLACK 45	BLACK 39	BLACK 53	BLACK 29	WHITE 23	BLACK 72

The forewoman: Divorced black woman, 51, works as vendor; said she "respects (Simpson) as an individual based on his past accomplishments"; said she had a "stressful, sick feeling" when she first heard Simpson was a murder suspect; described racial discrimination against blacks as a "somewhat serious problem"; lives in South Central Los Angeles.

A breakdown

Race: 1, 2

Gender: Men 2, Women 10

AP

Reasonable Doubts

Los Angeles (AP)

WHEN JURORS ACQUITTED O.J. Simpson of murder, they cited reasonable doubt about the evidence. The points of doubt raised most effectively by the defense are:

1. The Timeline:

The prosecution's minute-by-minute effort to reconstruct the killings of Nicole Brown Simpson and Ronald Goldman was designed to give Simpson enough time to commit the murders, return home, dispose of bloody clothes and a weapon, clean blood off his body and appear spotless and composed when a limousine driver met him. But the timeline provided only six minutes, from 10:55 P.M. when a shadowy figure was seen entering the house to 11:01 P.M. when Simpson emerged perfectly groomed. Jurors thought that was impossible.

2. The Vial of Blood:

Simpson's blood sample was drawn at the Los Angeles Police Department on June 13, 1994, the morning after the killings, but was not immediately booked into evidence by Detective Philip Vannatter. Vannatter had put it in his pocket and took it to Simpson's estate where criminalists were collecting evidence. Jurors questioned why he would have carried it around for hours instead of booking it. The defense suggested evidence planting.

The evidence

The prosecution and defense gave a few pivotal elements very different interpretations.

The lost minutes

Prosecution: O.J. Simpson lacked an alibi, or even a plausible story, for what he was doing between 9:36 p.m. and 10:40 p.m. Reports from neighbors of a wailing dog show the murders occurred around 10:15 p.m.
Defense: Simpson couldn't possibly have driven to Nicole Brown Simpson's home, killed two people, hid bloody clothes and a weapon, driven home, cleaned up and changed his clothes before greeting a limousine driver at 11 p.m.

DNA

Prosecution: The chances of matching characteristics in a blood drop found at the murder scene and blood from anyone other than Simpson are less than 1 in 170 million.
Defense: Faulty or corrupt evidence collection tainted the sample. Blood was planted in an attempt to frame Simpson.

A trail of blood

Prosecution: Simpson left bloody shoeprints and an extra large leather glove at the crime scene. In his rush to hide the second bloody glove, he dropped it behind his guest house. He also bled in his Bronco and in the foyer of his house.
Defense: Part of a conspiracy led by racist Los Angeles Police Detective Mark Fuhrman.

A violent past

Prosecution: Simpson was prone to jealous rages and had beaten Ms. Simpson repeatedly. This proved his motive.
Defense: Beatings were irrelevant, isolated events. The Simpsons had divorced amicably and moved on.

Simpson juror Brenda Moran speaks to the media in the parking lot of her attorney's office.

Photo Chris Pizzello

3. The Socks:

A pair of socks found on a rug next to Simpson's bed were collected by a criminalist who said he picked them up because they seemed "out of place." But no one noticed any blood on them until two months later when they were being examined at the crime lab. Defense experts said the blood may have been smeared on them when they were lying flat, not when a person was wearing them.

4. The Glove:

The most infamous piece of evidence in the Simpson trial was the glove found on a leafy pathway behind a guest house at Simpson's estate. Witnesses including Detective Mark Fuhrman said it was sticky with blood when they saw it some seven hours after the killings. Testimony suggested the blood would have been dry by then. Although the glove was analyzed as having large amounts of blood and trace evidence on its surface, the leafy area around it was pristine. Jurors asked why there were no blood drops on the pathway.

5. The Bronco:

Although scientific analysis uncovered traces of blood in Simpson's vehicle, the amounts were

Hordes of photographers, reporters and television cameras wait outside Simpson's estate the day after the verdict was announced.

Photo Paul Sakuma

small and most were not immediately detected. Some witnesses claimed they saw no blood at the outset, and photographs provided conflicting evidence of when blood was found on various parts of the vehicle.

6. The Absence of Blood in Simpson's House:

Although prosecutors claim he arrived home after walking through blood and dirt, there were no traces of blood or soil on the light-colored carpet in Simpson's house.

7. Mark Fuhrman's Testimony:

The since-retired police detective found much of the key evidence including the glove and the first Bronco stains. But his decimation by the defense as a racist and liar threw all of his testimony into doubt.

8. Simpson's Appearance and Demeanor:

Witnesses said that Simpson was fashionably attired and immaculate when he boarded a plane for Chicago, appearing as natty as an advertisement for men's clothing. His attitude was cheerful and he signed autographs for fans. When he returned the next day, after receiving news of his ex-wife's slaying, he was distressed.

Epilogue

Sylvia Woods, owner of the famed Sylvia's Restaurant, reacts after hearing the not guilty verdict of the O.J. Simpson trial at her restaurant in New York City's Harlem.

Photo Adam Nadel

WHEN SUPERIOR COURT JUDGE Lance Ito's clerk, Deirdre Robertson, read the jury's verdicts in the case of *The People v. Orenthal James Simpson,* the long trial that often seemed as surreal as the slow-speed chase that preceded it at last came to an end the morning of October 3, 1995, a year and a week after jury selection commenced.

But a new American journey had just begun, for the trial that had once unified a country, that had drawn us to our television sets and had us talking to friends, neighbors, co-workers and strangers, suddenly started tearing us apart, exposing a racial gulf the size of which surprised many.

In New York's Times Square, as the verdict reading was shown on the giant Sony Jumbotron TV, black spectators erupted in cheers and honked their car horns. Most whites remained subdued. At Howard University, a class of black

law students cheered. At the University of Utah College of Law, 85 percent of one mostly white class said he was guilty. And one picture in *Newsweek* captured it all: a group of students at Augustana College in Rock Island, Illinois, the black students applauding and leaping in joy, the white students frozen in stunned silence.

A black-majority jury of 10 women and two men reached a verdict after deliberating less than four hours. A nation that couldn't talk about the Simpson case enough struggled to understand why the jury hardly wanted to talk about it at all.

The verdict was not guilty on all counts in the murders of Ronald Goldman and Nicole Brown Simpson. To some people, that just didn't seem right; it seemed to them like a murderer buying an acquittal the way he bought his Ferrari, aided and abetted by a high-paid team of con men that duped a jury with a high-stakes form of three-card monte. To others, it was sweet justice, a long-overdue nationally televised example of the system finally doing for a black man reared in the projects what it's done for decades for white men raised in the suburbs. The battle lines were drawn, whites on one side, blacks on the other.

On Op-Ed pages, at street corners, in churches and offices, people struggled to make sense of it all. Even the president came forward, saying in a speech that the rift revealed by the Simpson case called for individual, and not government, solutions, with a new form of open conversation between whites and blacks. "This may seem like a simple request," said Clinton, "but for tens of millions of Americans, this has never been a reality. They have never spoken, and they have never listened."

Simpson shot an 82 on the par-72 Hombre Golf Course in Panama City Beach Fla., on October 17.

Photo Andrew Innerarity

THE O.J. SIMPSON TRIAL By the numbers

As of Thursday, Sept. 28

Cost of trial	**$8.9 million** (est.)
Days Simpson has spent in jail	**469**
Days jurors have been sequestered	**261**
Number of attorneys who have presented evidence in court	**D: 11** **P: 9**
Number of motions filed	**393 by both sides**
Exhibits presented duding testimony	**D: 369** **P: 488**
Books writen about the case	**9**
Chance blood drop at murder scene was left by a black or white person other than Simpson	**Less than 1 in 170 million**
Witness with the longest name	**Lakshmanan Sathyavagiswaran**
Letters Simpson received before publishing his book, "I Want to Tell You"	**300,000**
Hours CNN has aired the trial	**588**
Hours of trial coverage, commentary, commercials	**E!: 935** **Court TV: 685**
Money each juror earns each day	**$5**

AP

Jurors, breaking their silence one by one in TV news shows and in newspaper interviews, disputed that race had anything to do with their quick verdicts. The prosecution, they said, failed to prove its case beyond a reasonable doubt, presenting a case that lacked a motive, lacked credible police witnesses, and lacked gloves that would slip on Simpson's hands the way jurors thought they should.

"In plain English, the gloves didn't fit," said juror Brenda Moran, in a statement reminiscent of Johnnie Cochran Jr.'s closing theme: "If it doesn't fit, you must acquit." Another juror, Lionel "Lon" Cryer, said that he and other jurors had concluded there were many opportunities for contamination of evidence. "It was garbage in, garbage out," he said, again echoing a defense trial refrain.

The Simpson verdicts arrived, appropriately enough, at the peak of hurricane season, and they left America with a lot of cleanup to do. Pick an institution, any institution, and the Simpson case gave ample cause to examine and repair: the police, the jury system, the judiciary, the media. Look, also, at the moral issues: race

Denise Brown, right, Chair of the Nicole Brown Simpson Charitable Foundation, hugs Catherine McClary, president of Domestic Violence Project SAFE/House, at the Safe House Dedication on Sunday, October 8, 1995, in Pittsfield Township, Michigan.

Photo Linda Radin

relations truth, justice and dignity. All took their hits.

One of the first targets of attack after the trial was one that came under fire during the trial: the courtroom pool camera. Judges in big trials—the Susan Smith case, the Menendez brothers' retrial and the Selena murder trial—all decided to proceed outside the camera's stare. A movement to put cameras in federal courts took a big hit. Even one prominent member of the Dream Team, Gerald Uelmen, spoke of his concerns that the camera does more harm than good.

Attention turned, too, to the lawyers. As members of a profession so vilified that it could generate its own joke books, lawyers entered this trial at a distinct disadvantage. Critics like to note that nothing that happened during the trial, from Chris Darden's pouting to Johnnie Cochran's pounding, did anything to improve that reputation. By the end of the case, things got so bad that attorneys were arguing over whether a syringe was a syringe. The Bar of California drafted a set of attorney conduct rules, partly as a result of the case, and began investigating some of the attorneys involved in the Simpson case.

Investigators themselves came under investigation. Nowhere was the post-riot rift between whites and blacks more profound than in perceptions of the police. Where everyone did agree, if for different reasons, was that police had better clean up their act.

The Simpson trial proved that a jury could have zero tolerance for police racism. Jurors said they didn't acquit Simpson because of retired Detective Mark Fuhrman's racist views, but noted that Fuhrman's credibility as a witness plummeted. The police DNA lab may not quite be the "cesspool of contamination" the defense suggested, but it certainly has quality-control problems. At best, police technicians were sloppy. At best, detectives cut corners and stretched the truth. So much could have been avoided if police had just followed their own rules. If Detective Philip Vannatter had just booked the vial of Simpson's blood into evidence the way he was supposed to, rather than taking it back to Simpson's house where key blood evidence was found, the defense would have lost an entire line of cross-examination—and the jury would have had one less reason to acquit.

In the aftermath of the Simpson case, people were re-examining the jury system, the way jurors are selected, the extent to which juries represent the population, the manner in which juries consider evidence, and the issue of whether unanimous verdicts are necessary in criminal cases. Some even were saying the jury system was broken and that judges alone should hear evidence. But in the racially-charged Simpson aftermath, simply suggesting reforms to the jury system created more controversy, as blacks accused reform-promoting whites of whining over a verdict that didn't come out the way whites thought it should.

It's an awkward testimony to how deeply the Simpson case touched America that when we think of the aftermath of the trial we instantly think of ourselves. On verdict day, Fred Goldman, struggling to contain his emotions, spoke of his first nightmare, the day he found out his son had been murdered. Fred Goldman said he then experienced his second nightmare: sitting in court and listening to a jury acquit the man whom Goldman believes slashed his son's throat. The Goldmans have vowed to sue Simpson out of ever Hertz dollar he ever made; it was their only remaining weapon.

The family of Nicole Brown Simpson also filed a civil lawsuit against Simpson. They also had to work with him—or against him—to find a permanent home for Simpson's two youngest children, Sydney and Justin, placed in the cruelest of circumstances. Their mother was dead and their father was still believed by some to be the man who killed her. The Browns also had some fight left in them. They promised to continue to expose the horrors of the domestic violence that the jury said had nothing to do with Nicole's murder.

For the others involved in the case, their lives will be defined by the trial, their identities summed up in Simpson shorthand: The Limo Driver, The Maid, The Houseguest. But this being the land of opportunity, the Simpson case offered money to be made. Brian "Kato" Kaelin, the most inarticulate witness of the trial, was given his own talk-radio show. Tracy Hampton, supposedly so emotionally fragile that the judge had to seal the documents explaining why she resigned as a juror, was taking her clothes off for money for *Playboy*. Book publishers scrambled to sign up the jurors and the attorneys. Marcia Clark and Chris Darden both signed with the William Morris Agency. Two TV legal eagles, Greta van Susteren and Roger Cossak, parlayed their punditry into a new TV show.

And there are the victims, who throughout the trial, when they weren't an afterthought, certainly seemed an intrusion. It had become a cliché news assignment in the Simpson case to send a reporter to the victims' grave sites and write about how quiet it was. Most grave sites are. But the point is well-taken. Nicole Brown Simpson and Ronald Goldman are dead and

always will be and there's nothing anybody can do about it. That quiet you hear is the sound of money not being made, of lives not being lived. Whatever debate is raging, whatever legal reforms are enacted, it won't be heard at the graves.

And then there's Simpson. His world is shattered. The middle-aged white men he used to play golf with, and who gave him jobs selling rental cars and appearing in movies, are among those who most vehemently believe he's a killer who got lucky. His staunchest supporters are urban African-Americans, the folks who made up the bulk of his jury, and it's been a long time since Simpson has been to the community.

Simpson's early efforts to explain himself were a miserable—and highly public—failure; he agreed to a no-holds-barred live interview with NBC, then backed out when he found out the session wouldn't be a "conversation." He would then speak for free to the *New York Times*, but refuse to discuss the evidence, and again for pay to the *Star*, a supermarket tabloid, saying that the verdicts were a "miracle" but that life in a gilded cage on Rockingham was far from heavenly. "It's like I'm still a prisoner," he told the *Star*. "And I haven't really had a chance to grieve." He vowed to find the "real" killer or killers, and to spend more time with his children.

Still, as Simpson played the 72-par Hombre Golf Club course in Panama City Beach in mid-October, on his daughter's 10th birthday, there were reminders of the O.J. the world knew—or thought it knew—before the murders. Simpson smiled for video cameras, posed for pictures with women and stopped to sign autographs. "I have it on video. Pretty exciting, huh?" said

Diane Faust, who, when she heard about Simpson's golfing, grabbed her video camera and rushed to the links. "I said, 'Welcome to Panama City Beach, Florida,' and he said, 'I love it here.' "

Not everyone was so hospitable, however, in Simpson's first public appearance since the murder acquittals. When rumors circulated that local attorney Wes Pittman would sell his home to Simpson, the reaction was ugly. "I don't know how anyone else heard about it," he said. "We've got droves of people driving by our house. We've gotten threatening calls. Our neighbors are irate that we might sell to O.J. Simpson. Reports are rampant that we've received a down payment. Shoot, I haven't received a dollar."

MICHAEL FLEEMAN
Associated Press Writer
1995

Following page: Charlene Tilton, left, and Cindy Josten hold posters of murder victims Nicole Brown Simpson and Ronald Goldman, some of the more than 2,000 participants in a candlelight march held Saturday, October 7, 1995 in Los Angeles. The march was organized by the National Organization of Women.

Photo Eric Draper

9/19/12
13
1/19/07